ROUTLEDGE LIBRARY EDITIONS:
PHONETICS AND PHONOLOGY

Volume 10

SYLLABLE THEORY IN PROSODIC PHONOLOGY

SYLLABLE THEORY IN PROSODIC PHONOLOGY

JUNKO ITÔ

LONDON AND NEW YORK

First published in 1988 by Garland Publishing, Inc.

This edition first published in 2019
by Routledge
2 Park Square, Milton Park, Abingdon, Oxon OX14 4RN

and by Routledge
711 Third Avenue, New York, NY 10017

Routledge is an imprint of the Taylor & Francis Group, an informa business

© 1988 Junko Itô

All rights reserved. No part of this book may be reprinted or reproduced or utilised in any form or by any electronic, mechanical, or other means, now known or hereafter invented, including photocopying and recording, or in any information storage or retrieval system, without permission in writing from the publishers.

Trademark notice: Product or corporate names may be trademarks or registered trademarks, and are used only for identification and explanation without intent to infringe.

British Library Cataloguing in Publication Data
A catalogue record for this book is available from the British Library

ISBN: 978-1-138-60364-6 (Set)
ISBN: 978-0-429-43708-3 (Set) (ebk)
ISBN: 978-1-138-31756-7 (Volume 10) (hbk)
ISBN: 978-1-138-31759-8 (Volume 10) (pbk)
ISBN: 978-0-429-45512-4 (Volume 10) (ebk)

Publisher's Note
The publisher has gone to great lengths to ensure the quality of this reprint but points out that some imperfections in the original copies may be apparent.

Disclaimer
The publisher has made every effort to trace copyright holders and would welcome correspondence from those they have been unable to trace.

Syllable Theory in
Prosodic Phonology

Junko Itô

Garland Publishing, Inc. ■ New York & London
1988

Copyright © 1988 Junko Itô
All Rights Reserved

Library of Congress Cataloging-in-Publication Data

Itô, Junko.
Syllable theory in prosodic phonology / Junko Itô.
p. cm. — (Outstanding dissertations in linguistics)
Originally presented as the author's thesis (Ph.D. —University of
Massachusetts, 1986).
Bibliography: p.
ISBN 0-8240-5189-0
1. Syllabication. 2. Prosodic analysis (Linguistics) I. Title. II.
Series.
P235.I86 1988
414—dc19   88-16415

Printed on acid-free, 250-year-life paper
Manufactured in the United States of America

ACKNOWLEDGEMENTS

It has been my good fortune to have had Alan Prince, John McCarthy, Lisa Selkirk, and Mark Feinstein as members of my committee, without whose pioneering work on syllable structure the questions dealt with in this thesis could not even have been formulated. Their support and encouragement have been invaluable. I am especially indebted to my advisor Alan Prince, who first encouraged me to venture into phonology and whose influence on my work has been extensive throughout my graduate career. He has generously contributed ideas to this thesis, ranging from some of the central hypotheses to detailed questions regarding individual analyses. John McCarthy, my first phonology teacher at UMass, has guided me through this dissertation with his enthusiasm and wealth of ideas, which I hope have found some reflection in the pages that follow. My thinking about syllable structure has been profoundly influenced by Lisa Selkirk's writings. I am grateful for her comments and suggestions, which often clarified my vague initial ideas and turned them into clear hypotheses. Mark Feinstein, who was always willing to discuss incomplete drafts, contributed ideas and made many insightful suggestions.

I would also like to thank the UMass Linguistics faculty and students for many helpful discussions on linguistics and other matters, in particular Toni Borowsky, Roger Higgins, Yoshihisa Kitagawa, Angelika Kratzer, Kiyoshi Kurata, and Scott Myers. Special thanks to Armin Mester, who contributed substantially to this dissertation and provided constant encouragement.

This thesis is dedicated to my parents, whom I wish to thank for their love and confidence over the years.

TABLE OF CONTENTS

CHAPTER I. THEORETICAL FRAMEWORK

1.0 Introduction................................. 1

1.1 Principles of Prosodic Phonology
    1.1.1 Prosodic Licensing.................... 3
    1.1.2 Locality.............................. 7
    1.1.3 Directionality....................... 10

1.2 Structure Preservation and
    Prosodic Domains............................ 11
    1.2.1 Structure Preservation............... 12
    1.2.2 Prosodic domains and the
           phonological cycle................... 13

1.3 Appendix: The representation
    of the syllable............................. 14

CHAPTER II. CONDITIONS ON SYLLABIFICATION

2.0 Introduction................................ 17

2.1 The Problem of Locality..................... 17

2.2 Geminate Inalterability..................... 22

2.3 Conditions on Melody-Skeleton
    Association................................. 26

2.4 Positive and Negative
    Wellformedness Conditions................... 32

2.5 Case Studies

    2.5.1 Italian syllable structure........... 35
    2.5.2 Finnish syllable structure........... 40

2.6 Melody Constraints and
    Syllable Conditions......................... 44

CHAPTER III. CONTINUOUS SYLLABIFICATION
               AND STRAY ERASURE

3.0 Introduction................................. 48

3.1 Cluster Simplification in Diola Fogny

     3.1.1 Facts................................. 54
     3.1.2 Diola syllable structure.............. 58
     3.1.3 Nasal Assimilation as
            Melody Spread......................... 66
     3.1.4 Structure Preservation and
            Extraprosodicity...................... 69
     3.1.5 The Ordering versus the
            Continuous Hypothesis................. 74
     3.1.6 Triconsonantal cluster
            simplification........................ 77

3.2 Lardil Word Final Truncations

     3.2.1 Facts................................. 84
     3.2.2 Lardil syllable structure............. 86
     3.2.3 Word-level Phonology.................. 91
     3.2.4 Word-Level Extraprosodicity:
            Comparison with Diola................. 99

3.3 Attic Greek Consonant Loss

     3.3.1 Attic Greek
            syllable structure................... 103
     3.3.2 Word-Level Extraprosodicity
            and Stray Erasure.................... 111

CHAPTER IV. SYLLABIFICATION AND STRAY OPERATIONS

4.0 Introduction................................ 113

4.1 Ponapean Epenthesis......................... 120

     4.1.1 Ponapean syllable structure.......... 121
     4.1.2 Melody Spread and
            Stray Epenthesis..................... 131
     4.1.3 OCP Fusion........................... 134

4.2 Epenthesis in Sino-Japanese Morphemes....... 144

     4.2.1 Syncope versus epenthesis............ 146
     4.2.2 Quality of epenthetic
            vowels and epenthesis contexts....... 149
     4.2.3 Parameters and typology.............. 154

    4.3 Skeletal Rules and
         Syllable Structure......................... 155

    4.4 Concluding Remarks......................... 162

CHAPTER V. DIRECTIONALITY IN SYLLABIFICATION

    5.0 Introduction............................... 163

    5.1 Syllabification in Icelandic -
         a Case Study............................... 169

         5.1.1 Icelandic syllable structure......... 170
         5.1.2 Erasure and Epenthesis
                in Icelandic......................... 180
         5.1.3 Interaction of Epenthesis
                and Erasure.......................... 184

    5.2 Further Directionality Effects

         5.2.1 Epenthesis in two Arabic dialects.... 191
         5.2.2 Comparison with a
                skeletal rule approach............... 199
         5.2.3 Edge epenthesis...................... 204
         5.2.4 Syllabification and Epenthesis....... 207
         5.2.5 Temiar epenthesis.................... 213

    5.3 Concluding Remarks......................... 218

BIBLIOGRAPHY.. 220

CHAPTER I

THEORETICAL FRAMEWORK

1.0 Introduction

The recognition of the syllable as a prosodic constituent has led to a deeper understanding of various phonological processes related to syllable structure, and the advantages of a prosodic/nonlinear conception of the syllable over a linear model have been convincingly demonstrated in much recent generative work dealing with the subject (Kahn 1976, Selkirk 1978, Halle & Vergnaud 1978, Feinstein 1979, McCarthy 1979a,b, Prince 1980, Steriade 1982, Levin 1985, etc.). While the syllable has enjoyed its status as a structural unit for some time, I believe it has not yet faced the full responsibilities which such a status entails. Its recognition as a prosodic unit brings the syllable in line with other hierarchical structures such as the metrical foot, the phonological word and the intonational phrase, and it is therefore imperative that syllable theory maintain and adhere to certain principles and hypotheses inherent to Prosodic Phonology (Selkirk 1980, 1981, 1984b, McCarthy & Prince 1985, in preparation).

(1) Basic Principles of Prosodic Phonology

   I. <u>Prosodic Licensing</u>: All phonological units must be prosodically licensed, i.e., belong to higher prosodic structure (modulo extraprosodicity).

   II. <u>Locality</u>: Well-formedness of a prosodic structure is determined locally.

   III. <u>Directionality</u>: Phonological mapping proceeds directionally: left to right, or right to left.

Syllable theory couched within the framework of Prosodic Phonology must not only maintain these principles but must also avoid duplicating their effects. If syllabification is merely compatible with Prosodic Phonology, the statements in (1) would be reduced to descriptive generalizations. What is necessary is that they have the status of <u>operative principles</u> guiding syllabification.

The goal of this dissertation is to explore the workings of a syllable theory which is an integral part of Prosodic Phonology. It will be shown that theory-internal considerations and a variety of empirical arguments converge on a conception of syllabification as <u>continuous template matching</u> governed by <u>syllable wellformedness conditions</u> and a <u>directional parameter</u>.

1.1 Principles of Prosodic Phonology

The basic principles of Prosodic Phonology - Prosodic Licensing, Locality, and Directionality - support a particular theory of syllabification. We will now consider each principle in turn and show how it bears on the question of the proper statement and role of syllable structure in the grammar.

1.1.1 Prosodic Licensing

The principle of Prosodic Licensing requires that all phonological units belong to higher prosodic structure. Segments must belong to syllables, syllables to metrical feet, and metrical feet to phonological words or phrases. Apparent exceptions to Prosodic Licensing fall under the theory of Extraprosodicity, which allows edges of well-defined domains to be special. In stress systems, we often find that the final syllables are not counted for metrical rules. For syllabification, the conditions which hold at word-edges are typically different from those encountered word-internally: We find edge segments not conforming to syllable sonority and different types of _initial_ complex onsets and _final_ complex codas. We will consider Extraprosodicity to be another licensing mechanism on a par with prosodic licensing (e.g. by syllabification).

By requiring that each segment be syllabically licensed (modulo extraprosodicity), Prosodic Licensing ensures that a phonological string is exhaustively syllabified. We can understand the mechanism of Stray Erasure (extensively motivated in earlier nonlinear work, e.g. McCarthy 1979b, Steriade 1982, Cairns & Feinstein 1982, Harris 1983) as eliminating unlicensed material from the phonological string so that Prosodic Licensing is satisfied.

Two theories of syllabification, broadly known as the template-approach (Selkirk 1978, Halle & Vergnaud 1978, etc.) and the rule-approach (Kahn 1976, Steriade 1982, Levin 1985, etc.), have been contrasted in the literature. I will argue that a syllable theory that does not duplicate the effects of the independent principle of Prosodic Licensing must be some version of the templatic approach, where syllabification consists of mapping the phonological string to the syllable template of the language. A syllable template is a kind of wellformedness condition defining the possible skeletal sequences of a language, e.g. [CCVC] (see 1.4 for other views on how templates can be defined). There are also other universal as well as language-specific wellformedness conditions on syllable structure beyond the simple skeletal sequencing. One such condition is the Universal Core Syllable Condition (2), which requires a sequence of -C-V- to be universally analyzed as tautosyllabic. (The interpretation of conditions like (2) will be discussed in detail in chapter 2, see also chapter 5).

(2) Universal Core Syllable Condition (UCSC)

IF   C V
THEN   σ

('The sequence CV must belong to a single syllable.')

Language-specific wellformedness conditions, such as the coda conditions extensively discussed in chapter 2, typically place restrictions on the class of segments which can be mapped to a certain template position.

In such a template-approach to syllabification, syllable mapping can be identified with the universal association mechanism which is triggered by Prosodic Licensing and governed by the syllable templates and other wellformedness conditions of the language.

No such identification is possible in a rule-approach. Here the possible syllable structures of a language are only indirectly derived from the set of syllable-building rules such as those given in (3) posited in the phonology.

(3) a.
$$CV \longrightarrow \overset{\sigma}{\overset{/|}{CV}}$$

b.
$$\overset{\sigma}{\underset{VC}{|}} \longrightarrow \overset{\sigma}{\underset{VC}{|\backslash}}$$

The existence of an Onset rule (3a) and a Rime Rule (3b) determines that CV and CVC syllables are allowed. If further (iterative or noniterative) adjunction rules are given in the grammar, more complex types of syllables will result.

Notice that the Principle of Prosodic Licensing is superfluous if syllable-building rules are normal obligatory phonological rules which apply whenever their structural description is met. Syllabification then takes place not because of Prosodic Licensing but because the rules are obligatory. Since Prosodic Licensing is an independently motivated principle of Prosodic Phonology, this kind of redundancy is a serious problem for the rule-approach and constitutes an argument in favor of a template-based syllable theory.

A related question concerns the interaction between syllabification and phonological rules. Our hypothesis (defended in chapter 3) is that syllable mapping takes place continuously throughout the phonological derivation.[1] In the context of Prosodic Phonology, continuous syllabification merely reflects the fact that Prosodic Licensing is an operative principle triggering syllable mapping throughout the lexical and postlexical phonology.

1.1.2 Locality

The Principle of Locality requires local wellformedness of a prosodic structure. This means that the wellformedness of a syllable or a metrical foot is determined solely within the syllable or foot and is crucially not dependent on information outside of that structure.

Consider a language which only allows sonorants to be codas. In a template-approach, this can be stated as a wellformedness condition on codas (4) which blocks the mapping of an obstruent into template-final position.

---

[1] In assuming that the output of every phonological rule is subject to syllabification, I am following the model adopted at least implicitly in e.g. Selkirk (1978, 1980, 1984b), Halle & Vergnaud (1978), McCarthy (1979a,b), Clements & Keyser (1983), Harris (1983).

(4)   Coda Condition:

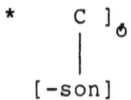

In a rule-approach, such a condition would be part of the structural description of the the syllable building rule which creates codas.

(5)   Coda Rule:

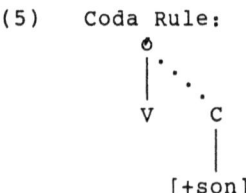

It would a priori seem that free syllable-mapping constrained by the Coda Condition (4) and the Coda Rule (5) are equivalent. In chapter 2, we will consider evidence relating to geminates which in fact distinguishes between the two approaches indicated above. I will argue that the principle of Locality can only be maintained if language-specific conditions are stated not over syllable rules but over syllable representations and are formulated as wellformedness conditions of the type given in (4). Such a condition on syllable structure presupposes the existence of a syllable template in the grammar. Hence the principle of Locality indirectly supports the templatic the principle of Locality indirectly supports the templatic approach to syllabification.

Locality also plays an important role in the domain of melody tier constraints. One type of melody tier constraint which is inherent to syllables is that of sonority.[2] Within a syllable, a segment constituting a sonority peak must be preceded and/or followed by a sequence of segments with decreasing sonority values. Sonority has both universal and language-particular aspects. Language-particular sonority requirements in most cases consist of minimum dissimilarity requirements on <u>adjacent</u> tautosyllabic segments (see e.g. Steriade 1982, Selkirk 1984). In our view, this limitation to melody adjacency is another consequence of the principle of Locality.

---

[2]Substantial work relating to sonority has been done in earlier phonological traditions (Jespersen 1909, de Saussure 1916, Grammont 1933) as well as in generative phonology (Hooper 1972, 1976, Bell & Hooper 1978, Kiparsky 1979, 1981, Selkirk 1984a, Steriade 1982, etc.).

1.1.3 Directionality

That phonological mapping is parametrized for directionality is considered uncontroversial in such areas as metrical theory (Hayes 1980, Prince 1983, etc.), root-and-pattern morphology (McCarthy 1979b, 1981), and reduplication (Marantz 1982, McCarthy & Prince 1985, in prep., Mester 1986).

I will argue that as a parameter available in Prosodic Phonology, directionality plays an explanatory role in Syllable Theory. A template-mapping approach to syllabification combined with the parameter on directionality can account for aspects of syllabification which were previously handled by positing certain extrinsic orderings of syllable-building rules (Steriade 1982). In particular, the directionality parameter makes it possible to map intervocalic consonants to the template in an unambiguous way. Right-to-left template mapping maximally incorporates segments into the onset and thus results in onset maximization (e.g. in Indoeuropean languages), whereas left-to-right mapping leads to coda maximization.[3]

Further consequences of the directionality parameter are found in epenthesis systems. It will be argued in

---

[3]Note that the Universal Core Syllable Condition (2) blocks an immediately prevocalic consonant from becoming a coda (see chapter 5 for discussion).

chapter 4 that epenthesis is best understood as degenerate syllable-mapping (i.e. forming syllables without vocalic nuclei, as in Halle & Vergnaud 1978, Selkirk 1981, and Lapointe & Feinstein 1982). In chapter 5, directional mapping will play a key role in correctly predicting the insertion sites in complex systems of epenthesis, providing further support for the directionality parameter in Syllable Theory.

1.2 Structure Preservation and Prosodic Domains

The operation of the Syllable Theory defended in this dissertation is in important ways determined by the principles and theoretical assumptions of Lexical Phonology (Pesetsky 1979, Mohanan 1981, Kiparsky 1982, 1983, 1984, Borowsky 1986). The principle of Structure Preservation (Kiparsky 1983) crucially relates to lexical and postlexical syllabification,[4] and the phonological cycle provides the domain in which the various principles of Prosodic Phonology are seen to operate.

---

[4]See Borowsky (1986) and Myers (1986) for consequences of Structure Preservation in English syllabification.

1.2.1 Structure Preservation

The principle of Structure Preservation (Kiparsky 1983) ensures that a wellformedness constraint (e.g. the constraint *[+voi, +son] ruling out the specification of (nondistinctive) voicing on sonorants) is not violated during the lexical phonology.

Since syllable templates and other conditions such as the coda conditions are also wellformedness constraints defined in the grammar, we can appeal to Structure Preservation to ensure that illformed syllables violating such syllable wellformedness conditions do not arise. Furthermore if syllable structures violating the conditions arise during the lexical cycles by the application of certain phonological rules, Structure Preservation triggers desyllabification, i.e. dissociation. (We will see such cases of desyllabification in chapter 3.) In the postlexical phonology syllable structures not conforming to the template or to other syllable conditions can be created, since Structure Preservation no longer holds (e.g. nondistinctive features can be introduced).

In order to be able to appeal to Structure Preservation in this way, the <u>structure</u> to be preserved must be defined in the grammar. It is interesting to note that this requirement is only met by a template-approach to syllabification and not by a rule-approach.

1.2.2 Prosodic domains and the phonological cycle

The phonological cycle plays an important role for the theory of Extraprosodicity and the operation of Stray Erasure. Our hypothesis is that the output of every cycle must be prosodically licensed and that Stray Erasure is invoked at the end of each cycle to eliminate unlicensed material. This is a very restrictive theory in that it eliminates all stray segments in each prosodic domain, except for extraprosodically licensed edge-segments.

Our hypothesis contrasts with a frequently-held view, according to which Stray Erasure applies at some level of derivation like the word level or the postlexical level. Convincing arguments have been made showing that segments must remain stray until late in the derivation (Steriade 1982). However, it is a notable fact that most of the arguments concern segments at the edges of morphological domains, which can be extraprosodically licensed and hence protected against Stray Erasure. I will argue in chapter 3 that edge-segments are universally extraprosodic during the lexical cycles and can be defined extraprosodic on a language-particular basis at the word level. Postlexically all segments must be syllabically licensed. I will show that these assumptions, together with the fact that Structure Preservation no longer holds at the postlexical level, provide the basis for an explanatory account of various Stray Erasure phenomena.

1.4 Appendix: The representation of the syllable

While most current researchers accept the existence of the level of syllabic terminals referred to as the skeleton mediating between the syllable and the melody, its exact representation is a matter of continuing debate. Kaye & Lowenstamm (1981) and Prince (1984) argue that the syllabic terminals are pure positional elements without any intrinsic content. The minimal characterization as C's and V's has been proposed by McCarthy (1979b) to account for the distribution of the vowels and consonants in the Arabic binyanim. Levin (1983) argues that the C's and V's are redundant and that the skeleton should in fact be considered timing units represented by X's. Hyman (1986) and McCarthy and Prince (1985) propose that the skeleton consists of weight units or moras.

There are further issues related to the nature of subsyllabic structure mediating between the syllable node and the skeleton. Many researchers recognize at least the subsyllabic constituents of Onset and Rime (Selkirk 1978, Halle & Vergnaud 1978, Steriade 1982 etc.). Others have proposed further distinctions: Margin, Nucleus, Coda

(Cairns & Feinstein 1982, etc.). Kiparsky (1981) proposes binary branching structures with sw nodes similar to metrical structures. Levin (1985) argues for a X-bar structure of the syllable where the maximal projection of the nuclear segment is equated to the syllable.

The nature of the skeleton and the form of subsyllabic organization are not independent of each other. With subsyllabic categories such as margin and coda, the information on the skeleton itself becomes unneccessary. In a model with no subsyllabic structures and the syllable node directly dominating the skeleton, more information on the skeleton is necessary.

The topics to be discussed in this thesis are mostly neutral with respect to these questions, and for purpose of exposition, I will adopt the representation proposed by Clements & Keyser (1983) given in (6) which recognizes the minimally necessary structure in representing quantitative and qualitative distinctions within a syllable.

(6)
```
                     σ       σ
                    /|\     /|\
     skeleton:    C V C   C V V
                  | |  \ /  |/
     melody tier: g a   k   o      gakkoo   'school'
```

It should be noted that unless explicitly discussed, nothing hinges on these details of representation. In the course of the discussion, I will freely use the descriptive terms nucleus, onset, rime, and coda to designate standard syllabic positions.

(7)

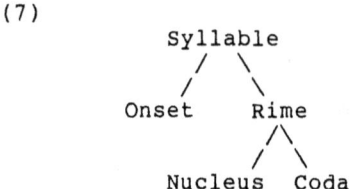

CHAPTER II

CONDITIONS ON SYLLABIFICATION

2.0 Introduction

The prosodic principle of Locality requires that the wellformedness of any prosodic constituent be determined locally, without making reference to external information about other structures. In this chapter, we will examine what at first glance appears to be a violation of the principle of Locality in syllable theory. It will be shown that the emerging theory of geminates in nonlinear phonology provides a solution to the problem which respects locality. The solution relies on the fact that the crucial information is expressed as part of wellformedness conditions on syllable representations rather than as part of the structural description of syllable-building rules.

2.1 The Problem of Locality

A representative sample of Japanese syllables is given in (1). The words in (1a) consist of open light syllables; open heavy syllables of type CVV appear in (1b); the

initial syllables in (1c) are closed with a nasal; the
words in (1d) contain syllables closed with obstruents,
and the final form <u>tootte</u> shows a maximal possible syllable
CVVC (superheavy syllable).[1]

(1)
    a.   ka.mi.ka.ze   'divine wind'

          i.ke.ba.na   'flower arrangement'

    b.   kai.soo   'seaweed'

    c.   sen.see   'teacher'

          kam.pai   'cheers'

    d.   sek.ken   'soap'

          gak.koo   'school'

          kap.pa   'legendary being'

          tos.sa   'impulsively'

          toot.te   'passing'

Each of the syllables in these words is of course
wellformed. If words consist of sequences of locally
wellformed syllables, then the free permutation of these
syllables should also result in phonologically wellformed
words of Japanese. Random permutations of the syllables
in (1) appear in (2). Some of the permutations constitute

---

[1] There are also superheavy syllables of the type CVNC in
the nonnative vocabulary, e.g. <u>ron.donk.ko</u> 'Londoner',
(I owe this example to William Poser (p.c.).

possible nonce forms (2a), whereas others are impossible in Japanese (2b).

(2) Free permutations of the syllables in (1)
    a.   ka.ze.mi
           see.sen
           soo.kai
           ba.ke.na
    b. * kap.toot
        * sek.pa
        * kap.sek
        * te.gak

The syllables in (2a) are vowel-final except for the final syllable in see.sen which is closed by a nasal. On the other hand, the forms in (2b) all include at least one syllable which is closed by an obstruent, and this is obviously the source of the trouble. Since the syllables in question stem from the grammatical examples in (1), their illformedness in (2) calls for an explanation. The difference is quite clear: In (1d) each of the syllables closed by an obstruent (sek, gak, kap, tos, toot) is followed by a syllable which starts with an identical obstruent (sek is followed by ken, kap is followed by pa, etc.), whereas in the ungrammatical forms

in (2b) this is not the case. The generalization can be
informally stated as follows:

(3)

An obstruent can be the final element in a syllable
only if the following syllable starts with an
identical obstruent.

Notice that in stating this generalization the principle
of Locality has in fact been violated. To determine the
wellformedness of a syllable we are dependent on
information outside of that syllable.

It might be expected that this problem of nonlocality
automatically disappears in nonlinear theory. The relevant
syllable representations are given in (4).

(4)
```
   a. kap.pa            b.  *kap.ta          c. *ta.kap
       σ     σ          *   σ     σ         *   σ     σ
      /|\   /|             /|\   /|            /|   /|\
      C V C C V            C V C C V           C V C V C
      | | \ / |            | | | | |           | | | | |
      k a  p  a            k a p t a           t a k a p
```

In the grammatical form kappa (4a), the single melody p
is linked to two C slots, representing its geminated
status. The other two forms *kap.ta (4b) and *ta.kap (4b),
which have no double linking, are ungrammatical. By making

use of the nonlinear conception of geminates, we can state the generalization about syllable-final obstruents somewhat differently:

(5)
> An obstruent can be a syllable-final melody only if it is simultaneously the syllable-initial melody of the following syllable.

This would correctly rule in (4a), where the melody p is both syllable-final and syllable-initial, and rule out both (4b) and (4c), where the melody p is purely syllable-final.

Steriade (1982) offers a syllable-based analysis for a similar phenomenon in Attic Greek, in which she proposes to place a <u>segmental linking condition</u> on the Coda Rule.[2] For the case at hand, we can formulate the condition as follows:

(6)
> An obstruent can be syllabified as a coda only if it is segmentally linked to the following C.

---

[2] We return to Attic Greek in chapter 3.

We have now given three different statements in (3), (5) and (6) to describe the situation. All three statements violate Locality and are plainly stipulative. The formulations in (5) and (6) use nonlinear vocabulary, but this should not obscure the fact that they still refer to the next syllable in order to distinguish between (4a) versus (4b&c). In terms of the principle of Locality there is so far no advantage to nonlinear theories, and to resolve this problem we must first take a closer look at the emerging theory of geminates.

2.2 Geminate Inalterability

It is well known that geminates have several distinctive properties which are directly captured by a nonlinear representation. The fact that they sometimes behave as two segments and sometimes as one segment falls out straightforwardly from the distinction between skeleton and melody tier.

(7)

```
    skeleton:      C   C
                    \ /
    melody:          k
```

Geminates acts as two units for rules referring to the skeleton but as one unit for rules referring to the melody tier.

There is, however, one other type of behavior that geminates exhibit: sometimes they unexpectedly resist the application of rules in spite of the fact that the structural description appears to be met (Kenstowicz & Pyle (1973), Guerrsel (1978), Schein (1981), Steriade (1982), Steriade & Schein (1984), Hayes (1986), etc.).

This phenomenon (which Hayes (1986) has dubbed Geminate Inalterability) and its implications for nonlinear theory were first pointed out by Schein (1981) and Kenstowicz (1982) with respect to the rule of postvocalic spirantization in Tigrinya.

(8) a. /ʔakal@b/ --> ʔaxal@b   'dog-pl' (@ = schwa)
                              (cf. kälbi 'dog-sg')
    b. /fäkkär-ä/ --> fäkkärä   'he boasted'
                     *fäxxärä
                     *fäxkärä

In (8a) the obstruent k becomes x, but in (8b) the geminate kk remains unspirantized, it is neither wholly spirantized as xx nor partially spirantized as xk, as might be expected.

The currently accepted generalization is that geminates are inalterable when two tiers are crucially involved in the rule. Hayes (1986) suggests that nonlinear theory offers a very natural explanation if the interpretation of association lines in structural descriptions is governed by the <u>Linking Constraint</u> given in (9).[3]

(9) <u>Linking Constraint</u> (Hayes 1986: 331)
Association lines in structural descriptions are interpreted as exhaustive.

In Hayes' (1986) formulation of Tigrinya Spirantization in (10), there is one and only one association line from the CV-skeleton to the melody tier. Therefore, the structural description is only met by a melody which is singly linked to the skeleton.

(10) <u>Tigrinya Spirantization</u> (Hayes 1986: p.336)

$$\begin{vmatrix} \bar{-}son \\ +ba\underline{c}k \end{vmatrix} \longrightarrow [+cont] \ / \ \begin{matrix} V & C \\ & | \\ & \underline{} \end{matrix}$$

The representation in (11a), but not that in (11b), satisfies the structural description.

---

[3]For further discussion and other approaches, see Steriade 1982, Archangeli 1985, Steriade & Schein 1984, to appear.

(11)
```
     a.                          b.
           V C                        V  C   C
           | |                        |   \ /
         /? a k a l @ b/            /f ä   k  ä r ä/

         ?axal@b  'dog-pl'          fäkkärä 'he boasted'
```

Since we are appealing to the double linking of the single velar melody in (11b) to block the Spiratization rule, we expect that in a representation with two singly-linked melodies like (12) the first k-melody should satisfy the structural description and undergo the rule.

(12)
```
        V    C  C
             |  |
             k  k
             ↓
             x
```

This prediction is borne out in Tigrinya by kk clusters arising across morpheme boundaries, which have the double-melody representation (12) (see Hayes 1986:336). Morpheme-internal geminates cannot have this structure because of the Obligatory Contour Principle (Leben 1973, Goldsmith 1976, McCarthy 1979b, 1981, 1986). The OCP in (13) ensures that the representation in (11b) is the only one possible for fäkkärä, where the geminate is morpheme-internal.

(13) <u>Obligatory Contour Principle</u> (OCP)[4]

      At the melodic level, adjacent identical elements are prohibited.

2.3 <u>Conditions on Melody-Skeleton Association</u>

Returning now to the problem of nonlocality that we encountered in the formulation of the Japanese syllable structure condition, I propose the condition on Melody-CV association given in (14).

(14) Japanese Coda Condition

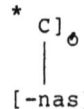

This condition, which disallows syllable-final nonnasal consonants, would seem to rule out even the wellformed cases of syllable-final obstruents as in <u>kap.pa</u>. The structural description of (14), however, involves a single association line between the skeleton and the melody, and according to the Linking Constraint the condition in (14)

---

[4]The OCP was first proposed for tonal phenomena in Leben (1973) and later extended to segmental phonology by McCarthy (1979b, 1981, 1986).

does not apply to forms with multiple association lines. In Hayes (1986), the Linking Constraint is only applied to the interpretation of structural descriptions of <u>rules</u>, but it is entirely natural and desirable to extend its coverage to all formal structural descriptions, whether they appear in <u>rules</u> or in <u>conditions</u>.[5]

The structural description of the condition on Japanese codas in (14) is only met when a nonnasal consonant is exhaustively linked to the syllable final C-slot. Thus the condition rules out the forms in (15b) and (15c) but not the form in (15a), where the obstruent melody p is doubly linked. In this way the geminate nature of p in (15a) protects it from being ruled out by the condition on codas.[6]

(15)
a. <u>kap</u>.pa   b. *<u>kap</u>.ta   c. *ta.<u>kap</u>

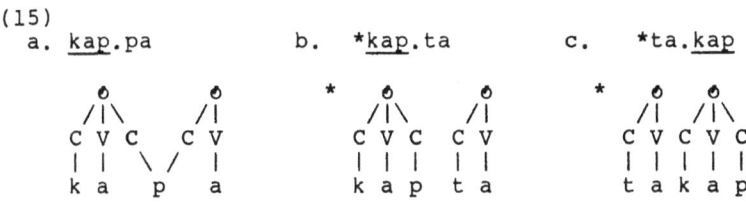

---

[5]I owe this idea to Alan Prince.

[6]There are several proposals in the literature on how to formally characterize Geminate Inalterability (Steriade 1982, Steriade and Schein 1984, to appear, Levin 1985). I have adopted Hayes' (1986) Linking Constraint because it most straightforwardly applies to filters and conditions. It is, however, possible to interpret the other accounts of Geminate Inalterability in the appropriate way.

The interest of this analysis lies not only in the way in which nonlinear representation is used to bring the Linking Constraint to bear on conditions. The crucial point is that the condition in (14) is stated in a strictly local way and refers solely to information internal to the syllable. The principle of Locality is therefore not violated. Of course, in cases like _kappa_, where the Linking Constraint makes condition (14) inapplicable, external information (in this case, the fact that _p_ is also linked to the onset C of the next syllable) still plays a role in the assessment of the syllabic wellformedness of the sequence _kap_, but crucially this information need only be available to the universal Linking Constraint and not to the language-particular syllable condition (14).

The Coda Condition (14), stated as a language-particular condition on _syllable representations_, offers an explanatory account of the properties of Japanese codas. Let us now consider whether a rule-approach can also appeal to the theory of geminates in a similar way by restricting the environment of a _syllable-building rule_. The relevant Coda Rule for Japanese is given in (16).

(16) Japanese Coda Rule

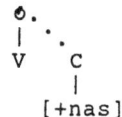

Rule (16) states that a skeletal C is syllabified as a coda only if it is exhaustively linked to a [+nas]. It turns out that (16) makes wrong predictions in two respects. First, it disallows all [-nas] codas without exception since obstruents will never fullfill the structural description of the rule, whether their melodies are singly or doubly linked. So the Linking Constraint does not help in the case of geminate obstruents, and the wellformedness of kappa remains unexplained. On the other hand, the Linking Constraint wrongly blocks the Coda Rule from applying if the [+nas] consonant is a geminate. As the examples in (17) show, nasal geminates are clearly permitted in Japanese.

(17)
    a. minna   'everyone'
    b. konničiwa   'good afternoon'
    c. amma   'masseur'

Let us systematically compare the Coda Condition (14) and the Coda Rule (16). There are four cases to be considered: singly linked [+nas] (18a), singly linked [-nas] (18b), doubly linked [+nas] (18c), and doubly linked [-nas] (18d).

(18)

   a. singly linked [+nas]   b. singly linked [-nas]

   c. doubly linked [+nas]   d. doubly linked [+nas]

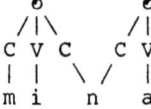 

Both the Coda Condition (14) and the Coda Rule (16) account for the difference in grammaticality between the singly linked cases: the grammatical (18a) versus the ungrammatical (18b). However, only Condition (14) correctly predicts the grammaticality of the doubly linked (18c) and (18d). Rule (16) wrongly predicts that neither (18c) nor (18d) is grammatical.

To remedy the situation, we might hypothesize that syllable-building rules are not subject to the Linking Constraint. The Coda Rule (16) could then syllabify both

(18a&c), but note that it would still not syllabify the nonnasal geminate (18d).

In the latter case, the relevant information would have to be encoded in the Coda Rule by using angled bracket notation as in (19).

(19) Japanese Coda Rule (revised)

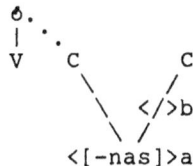

If a, then b.

This formulation of the Coda Rule is open to several criticisms. First, as a powerful mechanism which can relate any aspects of the phonological string the angled bracket notation is for principled reasons undesirable as a tool in the structural description of rules. Secondly, notice that the stipulated condition in angled brackets is an instance of the inalterability configuration, suggesting that a generalization has been missed. Finally, the formulation of the revised Coda Rule (19) is utilizing information outside of the syllable domain - a clear violation of the principle of Locality.

The Coda Condition (14) (repeated below in (20) does not face any of the above criticisms.

(20) Japanese Coda Condition:

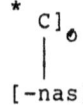

[-nas]

No angled brackets are involved, the theory of geminate inalterability gives us the correct interpretation without any stipulations, and the condition does not rely on information outside of the syllable and therefore poses no threat to the Locality Principle.

In sum, we have been able to uncover a clear advantage for a theory with conditions on syllable representations over a theory with conditions on syllable building rules.

2.4 Positive and Negative Wellformedness Conditions

In the analysis given above, the restriction on melody-to-skeleton association has taken the form of a negative condition. In this section, it will be shown that a negative filter is formally equivalent to a positive wellformedness condition.

All conditions, positive or negative, are implicational statements. For example, the Japanese Coda Condition (21), which disallows all nonnasal codas, can be rephrased as in (22).

(21)
$$* \quad \underset{[-nas]}{\overset{C]_\sigma}{|}}$$

(22)　　'If there is a syllable final consonant which is singly linked, its melody cannot be [-nas].'
　　　　　　　　or
　　　　'If coda and single link, then not [-nas].'

Since 'not [-nas]' is equivalent to '[+nas]', (22) can alternatively be expressed as (23).

(23)　　'If there is a syllable-final consonant which is singly linked, its melody must be [+nas].'
　　　　　　　　or
　　　　'If coda and single link, then [+nas].'

In syllable structure representation, this statement is the positive well-formedness condition below.

(24)
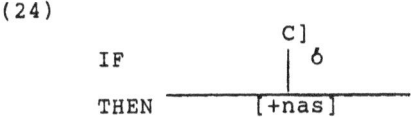

It is important to recognize the implicational structure of positive wellformedness conditions. Condition (24), for example, does not require all syllables to have nasal codas but is interpreted as follows: <u>If</u> there is a C-slot and a single link, <u>then</u> only when the melody is [+nas] can it be syllabified as a coda. If there is a double link, then the condition is simply not met, that is, the distinction [-nas] or [+nas] is irrelevant, and syllabification applies freely.

It should be noted that the positive condition (24) is not equivalent to the coda-building rule (25).

(25)

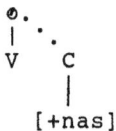

When the structural description is met, that is, when there is a C-slot which is singly linked to a [+nas], the positive condition (24) and the syllable rule (25) do the same work.

The difference arises when a phonological string does not meet the structural description. In such a case, the syllable <u>condition</u> is not effective and nothing restricts syllabification. On the other hand, the syllable <u>rule</u> simply does not apply. The consequences are crucially different: Syllabification takes place in the former case but not in the latter.

In order for the syllable rule to apply, it must be stated with the complicated disjunctions as shown in (19).

2.5 Case Studies

The special behavior of geminates in Japanese with regard to syllabification is by no means an isolated phenomenon, similar facts are found in many languages. We will consider the syllable structure analyses of two other languages, Italian and Finnish.

2.5.1 Italian syllable structure

The maximum syllable in Italian is CCVC, with two onset consonants and one coda consonant (Basbøll 1974, Vogel 1977, Chierchia 1982, 1983, Prince 1984). A word-medial triconsonantal cluster always consists of one coda consonant and two onset consonants as shown in (26).

(26)

in.flessibile	'inflexible'
al.tro	'other'
bur.gravio	'castle lord'
em.blema	'emblem'
es.presso	'express'

Sonority must rise in the onset so that the melody sequence in an onset cluster is always [-son][+son] (e.g. fl, tr, gr, bl).[7]

The consonants which appear in coda position in (26) are the sonorants and s. As (27) shows, obstruents other than s cannot occur in comparable positions.

---

[7]Word-initial sC sequences as in splendore or scrivere cannot be regarded as ordinary onsets but must be accounted for by a special mechanism. Chierchia (1983) gives two arguments that word-internal sC clusters in Italian must be considered heterosyllabic. Stressed vowels in open syllables are lengthened, but stressed vowels preceding sC clusters are always short (e.g. pasta), hence s must belong to the preceding syllable. A second argument is based on the observation that words like *pelsto or *persto are not possible. Since Italian syllables have only one postnuclear position, their ungrammaticality can be attributed to the fact that sC is not a possible word-internal onset.

(27)

    *it.flessibile

    *ap.tro

    *bud.gravio

    *eg.blema

    *ec.presso

However, obstruents are found in syllable-final position when they are part of a geminate:

(28)

lab.bro	'lip'
grap.pa	'brandy'
ap.plaudire	'clap, applaud'
tut.to	'all'
elet.trico	'electric'
rad.drizzare	'make straight, straighten'
ac.creditabile [kk]	'creditable'
ag.glomerare	'agglomerate'

Basbøll's (1974) characterization of the possible word-medial consonant clusters is given below with minor modifications (R = sonorants, and the subscripts indicate identity, cf. Basbøll 1974:35 for details).

(29)   V $\left\{\begin{matrix} C_i \\ s \\ R \end{matrix}\right\}$. C_i (R) V

The consonants permitted syllable-finally are the sonorants and <u>s</u>, and in addition the first part of any geminate consonant. This situation, although more complex, is clearly reminiscent of the Japanese syllable condition. I propose the condition on Italian codas in (30).

(30)   Italian Coda Condition:

$$* \; C \;]_\sigma$$
$$\begin{bmatrix} -\text{cont} \\ -\text{son} \end{bmatrix}$$

Condition (30), together with the maximum syllable template CCVC and the sonority requirements, gives the full range of predictions for the structures in (31).

(31)   a.   σ   σ
              /\   //\
              V C   C C V
              | | | | |
              a <u>l</u>   t r o   'other'

          b.   σ   σ
              /\   //\
              V C   C C V
              | | | | |
          *   a <u>p</u>   t r o

c.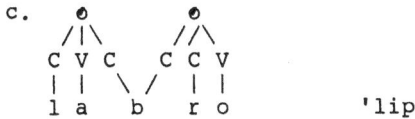
    l a b   r o   'lip'

The structural description of Condition (30) is not met in (31a) because l is [+son], and it is not met in (31c) because of the double link. The condition correctly rules out (31b), since an obstruent p is exhaustively linked to a syllable-final consonant.[8]

---

[8]There is one remaining problem for the formulation of the Italian Coda Condition in (30). As stated, the condition wrongly predicts that not only s but also f and š should occur ungeminated in coda position. We are faced with a dilemma because if the specification of [-cont] is omitted as in (i), singly linked s-codas are incorrectly ruled out.

(i)   Italian Coda Condition (revised)

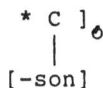

There is actually some support for this revised condition. Only sonorants (and not s) are allowed in word-final position, suggesting that the properties of s in word-initial, medial and final positions deserve a speicial and uniform treatment.

2.5.2 Finnish syllable structure

The syllable structure of Finnish allows one prenuclear consonant and up to two postnuclear consonants (Keyser & Kiparsky 1984, Prince 1984):

(32) CVCC-syllables
    a.   pyrs.tö
    b.   help.po

Sonority must decline from the nuclear vowel, as it does from r to s in (32a) and from l to p in (32b). The melody tier sequence is [+son][-son], the mirror image of Italian. The forms in (33) are disallowed because the sonority profile is violated in the first syllable.

(33)
    a.   * laps.ta
    b.   * uks.ta

The forms in (34) show that obstruents are possible codas whether they are single (34a) or geminated (34b).

(34) a.   lap.si   'child'
               uk.si   'door'
               lat.va   'top'
               jat.ka   'continue'

b. ha<u>t</u>.tu   'hat'

   pa<u>p</u>.pi   'priest'

   my<u>k</u>.kä   'mute'

The Finnish data in (32) - (34) do not warrant the postulation of a melody-to-skeleton association condition of the kind discussed for Japanese and Italian. Consider now the following paradigm, which illustrates the possible and impossible cases of two postvocalic consonants in the syllable.

(35)

a. pyr<u>s</u>.tö   'fish-, or bird-tail'

   kon<u>s</u>.ti   'trick'

   sal<u>s</u>.kea   'slender'

b. * pyr<u>k</u>.sö

   * tol<u>p</u>.kö

   * kon<u>t</u>.po

c. hel<u>p</u>.po   'easy'

   pol<u>t</u>.ta   'burn'

   tar<u>k</u>.ka   'exact'

   kyn<u>t</u>.tilä 'candle'

The syllable-final consonant can be s (35a), but plosive consonants are prohibited (35b) unless part of geminates (35c). This is the by now familiar constellation of facts, and the Finnish association condition is provisionally formulated in (36) to rule out singly-linked noncontinuants syllable-finally.

(36)
$$* \begin{array}{c} C\ ]_\sigma \\ | \\ [-cont] \end{array}$$

The condition above does not quite work because it would also rule out the grammatical examples in (34a). It is only when there are <u>two</u> postvocalic consonants that the restriction holds. We can add this specification to the condition on syllable-final consonant as in (37).

(37) Finnish Coda Condition:
$$* \begin{array}{c} C\ C\ ]_\sigma \\ | \\ [-cont] \end{array}$$

Condition (37) correctly singles out (38c) as ungrammatical.

(38)

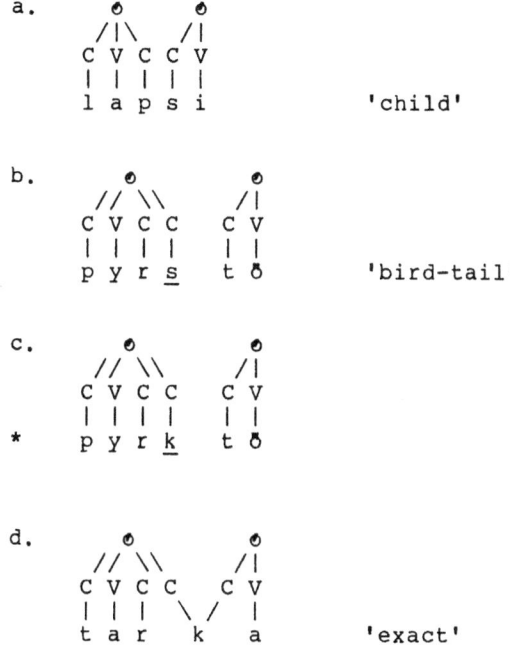

a. 'child'

b. 'bird-tail'

c. * 'exact' (pyrkto)

d. 'exact'

The forms in (38a,b,d) are not ruled out because in each case some part of the structural description of the Coda Condition (37) is not met: In (38a) there is only a single postvocalic C; in (38b) the crucial melody is [+cont], and in (38d) it is doubly linked.

2.6 Melody Constraints and Syllable Conditions

In order to explain the Finnish data considered above, Prince (1984:239) proposes the following sequential constraint on the melody tier.

(39)

　　　*[+cons][-cont][+cons]

This constraint rules out *pyrktö (38c) but allows tarkka (38d) because the melody tier only contains a biconsonantal cluster. Both this sequential analysis (39) and the syllable-based analysis proposed in section 2.5.2 crucially utilize the distinction between melody and skeleton, and they fare equally well in their descriptive coverage. The sequential constraint (39) uses intratier information, and the syllable constraint (37) repeated below in (40) uses intertier information.

(40)
$$* \begin{array}{c} C\ C\ ] \\ | \quad \sigma \\ [-cont] \end{array}$$

Let us then compare these two solutions with respect to the priniciple of Locality. Such a comparison requires that the definition of Locality be made more precise.

When we are dealing with syllables, it is clear that the relevant local domain is the domain of the syllable. On a single tier, however, it is reasonable to assume that Locality should limit the window which is available for scansion to two adjacent units on that tier.[9] The sequential constraint in (39) then violates melody tier locality in that it requires the simultaneous scansion of <u>three</u> elements, but the syllable condition (40) is stated locally within the syllable.

This does not mean that all melody constraints should be reformulated as syllable conditions (see e.g. Prince 1984, Itô 1984, McCarthy 1985, Mester 1986). Certain intersyllabic melody constraints are only made unenlightening by reference to syllable structure. Another melody constraint (41) discussed by Prince (1984) is a case of this kind. In Finnish, no nongeminate obstruent cluster may end in p, that is, *tp, *kp, *sp are ungrammatical.

(41)   * [-son] p

The constraint in (41) respects melody tier locality, and there is no advantage in stating this as a syllable structure constraint. Such a constraint would have to

---

[9]Notice that a window of this size is also implicit in the statement of the OCP.

say that an obstruent cannot be a coda if the following onset is p:

(42)
$$*\ \mathrm{C}]_\sigma\ \ _\sigma[\mathrm{C}$$
$$\quad\ \ |\qquad\ \ \ |$$
$$\ [-\text{son}]\quad\ \text{p}$$

In this case the syllable information is not only redundant but harmful in that it violates syllable locality. Thus the analysis consistent with Locality turns out to be the syllable solution for the triconsonantal case and the melody solution for the biconsonantal case.

Factors other than Locality also play a role in choosing between competing analyses. The phonotactic generalization for languages allowing only geminates to close their syllables can be stated as a constraint on the melody tier (Prince 1984).

(43)   *[+cons][+cons]

Notice that this melody tier constraint, although similar, cannot be identified with the OCP. The OCP requires that there are no adjacent <u>identical melody</u> sequences while the sequential constraint (43) ensures that there are no consonant sequences at all. Thus (43) blocks <u>nonidentical</u> consonant sequences such as *<u>tp</u>, *<u>kt</u>, *<u>ps</u> as well as sequences of identical melody elements like *tt, *pp, *kk, which are independently ruled out by the OCP. A syllable condition along the lines pursued in this chapter can be formulated as in (44) to account for the same set of facts.

(44)
$$* \quad \begin{array}{c} C]_\sigma \\ | \\ [+cons] \end{array}$$

This condition disallows all singly-linked consonants in the syllable coda but allows doubly-linked (geminate) consonants to close the syllable, exactly the situation we wish to characterize.

The syllable condition (44) is more desirable than the melody constraint (43) since it avoids a partial duplication of the effects of the universal OCP and makes it possible to maintain the restrictive hypothesis that no language-particular (non)identity requirements can be stipulated in the grammar.

CHAPTER III

CONTINUOUS SYLLABIFICATION AND STRAY ERASURE

3.0 Introduction

In this chapter, we will consider the syllabification and the syllable-related phonology of three typologically diverse languages: Diola Fogny (West African), Lardil (Australian), and Attic Greek (Indoeuropean). All three cases have previously been analyzed in a nonlinear framework (Steriade 1982, Wilkinson 1986), and in each case Stray Erasure of unsyllabified segments plays a crucial role. I follow Steriade (1982) in hypothesizing that all consonant deletions are the result of Stray Erasure of unsyllabifiable segments.

It is convincingly demonstrated in Steriade (1982) that syllabification takes place at various points during the cycle, intermingled with other phonological rules. There are two ways of implementing this important insight in Syllable Theory. One possibility is the Ordering Hypothesis defended in Steriade (1982), where the interactions between syllabification and phonological rules are captured by language-particular extrinsic ordering stipulations which arrange the order of syllabification rules and other phonological rules. Another possibility is the Continuous Syllabification Hypothesis pursued here and often tacitly assumed in other work (Selkirk 1978, Halle & Vergnaud 1978, McCarthy 1979, Clements & Keyser 1983, etc.), under which syllabification is always potentially applicable, hence also applicable after certain phonological rules.

I will argue that syllable conditions of the type developed in chapter 2, coupled with the basic assumptions and principles of Lexical Phonology and Prosodic Phonology, allow us to maintain the Continuous Syllabification Hypothesis.

The two central assumptions of our Syllable Theory which will play a key role in this chapter are the following (see also chapter 1 and chapter 2):

(1) a. Language-specific syllabification conditions are stated in terms of wellformedness conditions.

b. Syllabification is not performed by a set of language-specific rules but by the universal association mechanism (which includes initial association as well as reassociation and dissociation).

The principle of Structure Preservation ensures that all lexical conditions, including those of syllable structure (1a), are respected during the lexical phonology

(Kiparsky 1983). The principle of Prosodic Licensing
ensures the application of the syllabification mechanism
(1b) since the output of each phonological cycle must be
exhaustively syllabified (modulo Extraprosodicity, see
below). Unlicensed segmental material is subject to Stray
Erasure.

The interaction of these principles can be illustrated
by a simple hypothetical example. Consider a form like
kapta in a language with a coda condition such as (2),
which disallows obstruent codas.

(2)

This language-specific coda condition (2) is enforced
through the universal principle of Structure Preservation,
blocking syllabification of p in (3). The Prosodic
Licencing Principle disallows the prosodically unlicensed
p, which is subject to Stray Erasure.

(3)

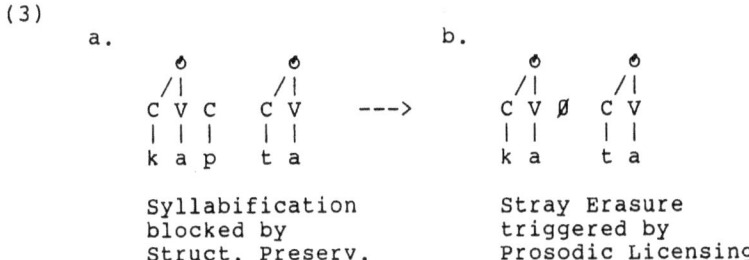

     a.   b.

     Syllabification   Stray Erasure
     blocked by   triggered by
     Struct. Preserv.   Prosodic Licensing

As discussed in chapter 2, syllabification of p is not blocked in a form like kuppe because of the doubly-linked structure. An interesting situation arises with a structure like (4a), which might arise by a vowel deletion rule.

(4)

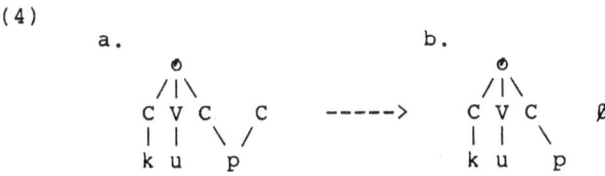

     a.   b.

Since the final consonantal slot cannot be prosodically licensed, it is stray-erased as shown in (4b). Notice that this application of Stray Erasure turns the p into a singly-linked coda obstruent (5a). Such a singly-linked coda obstruent violates Structure Preservation and is immediately dissociated from the syllable (5b). Prosodic Licensing in turn triggers Stray Erasure of p (5c).

(5)

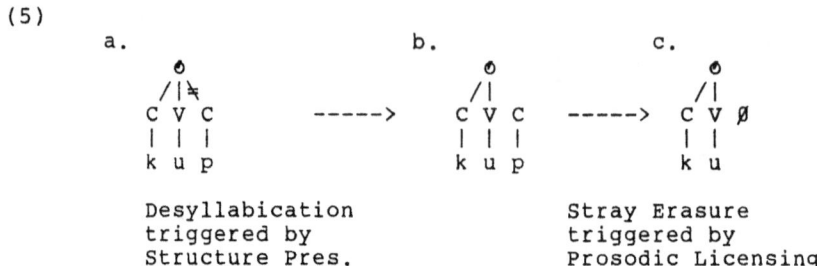

Thus Structure Preservation both blocks syllabification (3) and triggers desyllabification (5), ensuring that the syllable structure conditions of the language are not violated during the lexical phonology.

The principle of Structure Preservation holds during the lexical phonology but not in the postlexical phonology, where nonunderlying segments may be derived by allophonic rules. The principle of Prosodic Licensing, on the other hand, holds throughout the lexical and postlexical phonology. This difference in domain of operation makes further interesting predictions. Postlexically, since Structure Preservation no longer holds, syllable structure need not respect language-specific conditions.[1] The syllabification mechanism triggered by Prosodic Licensing can therefore create lexically illformed syllables. In this way we can avoid attributing the difference between

---

[1] Borowsky (1986), in an extensive analysis of English phonology, achieves highly interesting results from similar considerations.

lexical and postlexical syllabification to a difference in types of syllable-rules: the interaction of the universal principles (Association, Structure Preservation and Prosodic Licensing) and the language-specific syllable conditions determines the syllabification in the correct way without further stipulation.

An additional factor which enters in interesting ways into the derivational establishment of syllable structure is Extraprosodicity. In Prosodic Phonology, there are two ways in which segments can be licensed: by syllabification or by extraprosodicity. At the postlexical level (or at some level late in the phonological component before phonetic interpretation), all segments must be <u>syllabically</u> licensed, that is, the option of allowing edge segments by Extraprosodicity is no longer available. We will argue that extraprosodic licensing is universally operative during the lexical phonology and universally absent during the postlexical phonology; its availability at the word level is subject to parametric variation.

The overall goal of this chapter is to show how the interaction of continuous syllabification with lexical conditions on syllable structure, phonological rules, and Stray Erasure is controlled by the principles of Lexical Phonology and Prosodic Phonology.

3.1 Cluster Simplification in Diola Fogny

Diola Fogny, a West African language described by Sapir (1965), shows interesting interactions between a pervasive process of cluster simplification and a nasal assimilation rule. The Diola facts have given rise to a number of analyses. Kiparsky (1973) proposes an account in terms of the Elsewhere Condition, and Steriade (1982) presents a syllable-based analysis in which cluster simplification is the result of Stray Erasure and not an independent rule. I will here develop the syllable-based analysis in certain directions and show how the principles of Prosodic and Lexical Phonology interact under the Continuous Syllabification Hypothesis.

3.1.1 Facts

Cluster simplification takes place in Diola whenever certain consonant combinations arise through morpheme concatenation: In (6), obstruents (6a), sonorants (6b), and nasals (6c) are deleted.[2]

---

[2] There is a pervasive system of tense/lax vowel harmony in Diola (Sapir 1965, Kiparsky 1983). Lax vowels are transcribed here as /a, e, i, o, u/ and tense vowels as /ạ, ẹ, ị, ọ, ụ/. There are no neutral vowels.

(6) $C_1C_2 \longrightarrow C_2$

a. /let-ku-jaw/ --> lekujaw 'they won't go'
   /ujuk-ja/ --> ujuja 'if you see'
   /-kob-kob-en/ --> kokoben 'yearn, long for'

b. /-tey-tey-or/ --> teteyor 'disentangle'
   /jaw-bu-ɲar/ --> jabuɲar 'voyager'

c. /na-lañ-lañ/ -> nalalañ 'he returned'
   /na-yoken-yoken/ -> nayokeyoken 'he tires'
   /na-wañ-aam-wañ/ -> nawañaawañ 'he cultivated for me'

When a triconsonantal cluster (7) arises, the first two consonants are deleted, leaving only the final consonant.

(7) $C_1C_2C_3 \longrightarrow C_3$

/e-rent-rent/ --> ererent 'it is light'
/na-mañj-mañj/ --> namamañj 'he knows'

Although the forms cited in (7) may appear to be partial CV reduplication, it is quite clear that reduplication in Diola is of the whole morpheme type (cf. (6c) nayokeyoken), hence the first two consonants in the cluster must actually be elided in the phonology.

According to Sapir (1965:16) nasals assimilate to the place of articulation of an immediately following obstruent (8a) or nasal (8b). The resulting assimilated clusters are not simplified.

(8)
    a. /ni-gam-gam/ --> nigaŋgam 'I judge'
         /ku-boɲ-boɲ/ --> kubomboɲ 'they sent'
         /na-tiiŋ-tiiŋ/ --> natiintiiŋ 'he cut through'
         /pan-ji-manj/ --> paɲjimanj 'you.pl. will know'
         /ni-ceŋ-ceŋ/   --> niceɲceŋ 'I asked'

    b. /ni-maŋ-maŋ/ --> nimammaŋ 'I want'
         /ni-ɲan-ɲan/ --> niɲaɲɲan 'I cried'

Nasals are not simply immune from deletion; for example, the nonassimilated nasals in (6c) are elided. Kiparsky (1973:98) argues that the Elsewhere Condition is crucial for the formal expression of Sapir's (1965) verbal generalization "delete if not assimilated" and proposes the following rules, which stand in an Elsewhere relation.

(9)

    a. Assimilation (simplified)

$$\begin{matrix}C\\ [+nasal]\end{matrix} \longrightarrow [\ a\ place\ ]\ /\ \underline{\quad}\ [\ a\ place]$$

    b. Deletion (simplified)

$$C \longrightarrow \emptyset\ /\ \underline{\quad}\quad \left\{\begin{matrix}C & (i)\\ CC & (ii)\end{matrix}\right\}$$

"The inputs to [...] the Assimilation Rule are proper subsets of the inputs to branch (i) of the Deletion Rule. Therefore, by the Elsewhere condition, Assimilation will be disjunctive with branch (i) of Deletion. The rules now say: <u>assimilate, and if assimilation is inapplicable, delete</u>. (Kiparsky 1973:98)"

    The problematic aspect of this analysis is the disjunction in the Deletion Rule (9b). Branch (ii) of the rule is necessary to account for the triconsonantal cases in (7), where the initial nasals in the clusters have assimilated, but Deletion still applies. It is therefore essential that branch (ii) of Deletion (9b) is <u>not</u> in an Elsewhere relation with Assimilation (9a). Although written as one rule, the Deletion Rule (9b) consists of two unrelated branches whose similarity is merely accidental. We will give a unified syllable-based account of the triconsonantal cases in section 3.1.6 by appealing to Structure Preservation during the lexical derivation.

3.1.2 Diola syllable structure

The surface consonant combinations allowed in Diola Fogny are NC (nasal + obstruent), NN (nasal + nasal), and RC (liquid + obstruent). NC appears word-initially (10), word-internally (11), and word-finally (12). NN and RC occur only word-internally (13)-(14). In Diola only nasals can occur as geminates. The initial nasals in a word-initial cluster (10) are syllabic consonants.

(10) # NC...

   m̩.bur   'bread' (a Wolof loan)

   m̩.bi   emphatic mood

   m̩.ba   'or'

   n̩.daw   'a man's name'

(11) #...NC...#

   kaŋ.kan   'made'

   e.kum.bay 'the pig'

   jen.su   'undershirt'

   kun.don   'large rat'

(12) ...NC #

    famb   'annoy'

    ka.band   'shoulder'

    bunt   'lie'

    aŋkaŋk   'hard'

    kaŋg   'be furthest away'

    mañj   'know'

(13) #...NN...#

    ni.nen.nen   'I placed'

    ni.ŋaŋ.ŋan   'I cried'

    ni.ñañ.ñañ   'I rub arms'

    ni.mam.maŋ   'I want'

(14) #...RC...#

    sal.te   'be dirty'

    ar.ti   'negative suffix'

The NC combinations (10)-(12) are all homorganic clusters, and the NN combinations (13) are always geminates. Sapir (1965:8) notes that the only attested RC combinations are /-rt-/ and /-lt-/ with the same coronal place of articulation. /r/ actually alternates with /d/ in certain environments (e.g. d_{are} ~ r_{are} 'within'). Thus we can make the generalization that the members of all surface consonant clusters have identical place of articulation.

Except for the word-final syllable, Diola syllable structure allows no more than one consonant in either the onset or the coda, and word-internal consonant clusters are always heterosyllabic. The syllable template for Diola is given in (15).

(15) Diola syllable template : [C V V C]

Consider then the cases where cluster simplification takes place.

(16)
    a.   /ujuk-ja/   --> ujuja   'if you see'
    b.   /let-ku-jaw/ --> lekujaw 'they won't go'
    c.   /-kob-kob-en/ --> kokoben 'yearn, long for'

The syllabification of (16a) according to the Diola syllable template in (15) is given in (17).

(17)
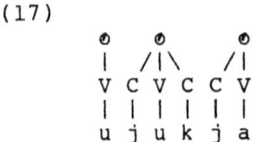

In order to subsume the loss of the medial k under Stray Erasure, the consonant must be blocked from being syllabified as a coda. I propose (18) as a lexical coda condition, disallowing syllable-final consonants.[3]

(18) Diola Coda Condition:

Because of Structure Preservation, the existence of this lexical constraint in the grammar entails that syllabification of the medial k in (17) is not possible during the lexical phonology. However, Prosodic Licensing requires that the output of every cycle be exhaustively syllabified. The language-specific coda condition (18) and the two universal principles, Structure Preservation and Prosodic Licensing, ensure the application of Stray Erasure as shown in (19).

---

[3]I assume that glides in Diola are [+cons] since they also delete, as shown in (6b). This might seem problematic and lead us to consider an alternative analysis of Diola syllable structure in which the syllable template itself is specified as containing no codas. But notice that the cases with geminates (13) and assimilated clusters ((11), (14)) constitute overt evidence for the existence of a coda and cannot be analyzed with a codaless template.

(19)

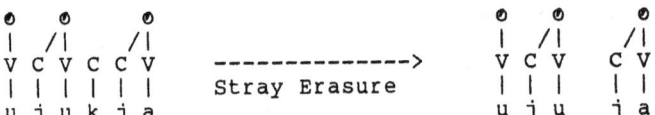

In a word like ku**ñ**ilak 'the children', where no consonants are lost, the Coda Condition (18) also blocks the final segment k from being syllabified as shown in (20).

(20)

Stray Erasure, however, does not apply to the final unsyllabified k because of Extraprosodicity. Recall that segments can be licensed in two ways: by syllabification and by extraprosodicity. Although not syllabically licensed, the final k is immune to Stray Erasure, being at the edge of the prosodic domain and therefore extraprosodically licensed.

(21)

   'the children'

As discussed in chapter 2, the Coda Condition as stated in (18) does not apply to doubly-linked structures, and the first part of a geminate can be syllabified because the structural description of (18) is not met.

(22)    'I want'

Consider now the cases in (23) where, given what we have said so far, Stray Erasure would also operate, resulting in ungrammatical forms.

(23)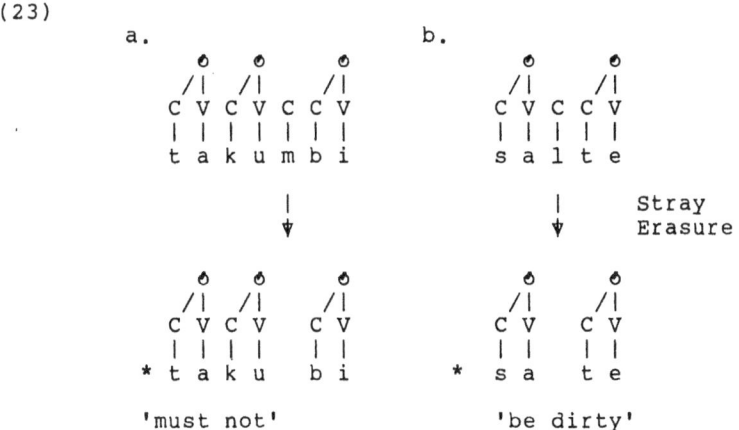

The solution to this problem lies in identifying further tier structure beyond the melody and the skeleton.

We have seen that the allowed consonant clusters in Diola are either homorganic clusters or nasal geminates (10)-(14). Substantial evidence and arguments have been given in the literature for the idea that homorganic clusters should be treated as partial geminates (Tuller 1981, Steriade 1982, Prince 1984, Hayes 1986b). Essentially following Steriade's (1982) analysis of Diola, I will assume that there is a separate manner tier distinct from the melody.

(24)

Manner tier:	[+nas]	[+lat]
	|	|
Skeleton:	C V C V C C V	C V C C V
	| | | | \/ |	| | \/ |
Melody tier:	t a k u b i	s a t e
	takumbi-	salte
	'must not'	'be dirty'

Since the consonants are doubly-linked in this representation, the structural description of the Coda Condition (18) is no longer met, and coda syllabification can take place as in (25). In order to avoid irrelevant association lines, I will henceforth use the notation N and L for a skeletal slot associated to [+nasal] and [+lateral], respectively.

(25)

The combination of the two factors: Extraprosodicity and double linking accounts for the word-final consonant clusters in (12), which consist of homorganic (i.e. linked) nasal-obstruent sequences.[4]

(26)

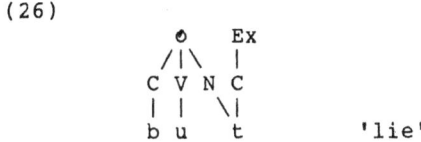   'lie'

---

[4]This is in all relevant respects Steriade's (1982) explanation of the phenomenon, recast in the framework of a different syllable theory: The penultimate consonant can be syllabified as a coda because it is doubly-linked.

3.1.3 Nasal Assimilation as Melody Spread

Diola Nasal Assimilation is formulated autosegmentally as Melody Spread in (27).

(27) Melody Spread

$$
\begin{array}{ll}
\text{Manner tier:} & [\text{+nasal}] \\
& | \\
\text{Skeletal tier:} & C_1 \cdots C_2 \\
& | \\
\text{Melody tier:} & [aF]
\end{array}
$$

sonority of $C_1 \geq$ sonority of C_2

The nasal assimilates to an obstruent or to another nasal, but does not assimilate to a liquid or glide. I assume that assimilation in Diola is governed by sonority (as argued by Hankamer and Aissen (1974) for Pali, a middle Indic dialect) and that a segment only assimilates to another segment with less or equal sonority.

Melody Spread (27) applies in a feature-filling way in underived environments and in a feature-changing way in derived environments. A feature-changing application is shown in (28b), where the coronal [t] spreads into the preceding nasal, displacing the labial specification of [m].

(28)

```
       a.                    b.                         c.
         [+nas]                [+nas]                     [+nas]
          |          Melody     |           Stray          |
       CVCVC - CV    Spread   CVCVC.  CV   Erasure      CVCVC CV
       |||||   ||    ----->   ||||‡ .||   ------>      ||||  \||
       najum   to             najum   to               naju   to

       '(he) stopped there'                            najunto
```

The delinked segmental melody is stray-erased, and the resulting structure (28c) contains a single melody unit doubly-linked to two skeletal slots.

Where Melody Spread (27) has applied, the double link makes the Coda Condition (18) ineffective, and the initial consonant in an assimilated biconsonantal cluster can be syllabified as a coda.

The syllabification of /let-ku-jaw/ 'fut.neg. -3 pl.-go' and /ni-gam-gam/ '1 sg.-judge' is illustrated in (29). The final consonants are extraprosodic, and the Coda Condition (18) disallows syllabification of the medial m in (29a) and t in (29b).

(29)

```
              a.                              b.
Syllab:       σ    σ    σ  Ex               σ    σ    σ  Ex
             /|   /|   /|  |               /|   /|   /|  |
             C V  C V C C V C              C V C C V C V C
             | |  | | | | | |              | | | | | | | |
             n i  g a m g a m              l e t k u j a w
```

(29cont.)   a.   b.

Melody
Spread:
```
           σ    σ      σ Ex
          /|   /|     /| |
          C V  C V  C C V C
          | |  | |  |≠\| | |
          n i  g a  m g a m              inapplicable
```

Syllab:
```
           σ     σ      σ Ex
          /|   /|\    /| |
          C V  C V N  C V C
          | |  | | \| | |
          n i  g a m  g a m              blocked by
                                         Structure Pres.
```

Stray Erasure
```
           σ     σ      σ Ex            σ    σ      σ Ex
          /|   /|\    /| |              /|   /|\   /| |
          C V  C V N  C V C             C V  C V C C V C
          | |  | | \| | |               | |  | | | | | |
          n i  g a ∅  g a m             l e ∅ k u j a w
```

         nigaŋgam   lekujaw

In (29a) Melody Spread (27) applies, and g becomes
doubly-linked. As soon as the double link is established,
the structural description of the Coda Condition is no
longer met, so that the skeletal slot can become part of
the coda. Melody Spread is inapplicable in (29b), and
syllabification of the medial t is still blocked by
Structure Preservation. In order to satisfy Prosodic
Licensing, Stray Erasure eliminates the unlinked melody
m in (29a) and both the skeletal slot and the melody t
in (29b).

3.1.4 Structure Preservation and Extraprosodicity

As discussed in the introduction to this chapter, Extraprosodicity is no longer operative at the postlexical level, and all segments must be **syllabically** licensed. This raises the question why Stray Erasure does not delete the final consonants postlexically as in (30).

(30)

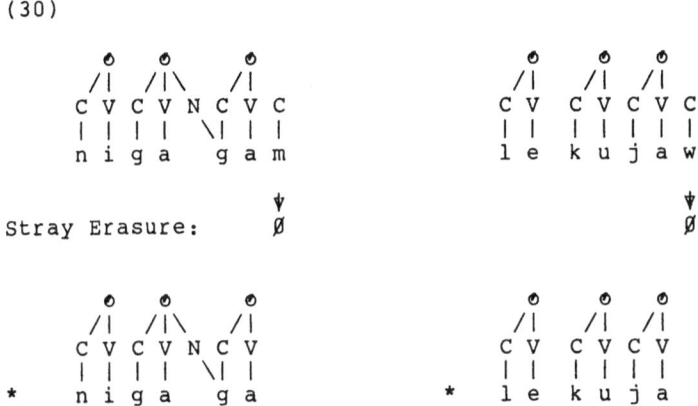

Stray Erasure:

But recall that the postlexical phonology has a second important property: Structure Preservation no longer holds, and consequently lexical wellformedness conditions are no longer enforced. Nothing therefore blocks the association of the final segment into the final syllable.

(31)

Notice that we do not have to say that the Coda Condition in particular is turned off postlexically - rather, it is the general principle of Structure Preservation which is no longer operative, an assumption which is well motivated in the theory (Kiparsky 1983).

The fact that Structure Preservation does not hold postlexically has a second important consequence: The Diola syllable template (15), itself a lexical condition, is no longer enforced. We can therefore adjoin previously extraprosodic consonants to the final syllable even if the syllable template is already filled, resulting in syllables with two coda consonants at word-edges as in (32b).

(32)

    a. <u>Lexical</u>   Structure Preservation and Extraprosodicity

b. <u>Postlexical</u> No Structure Preservation and no
              Extraprosodicity

The full cyclic derivation of the compound /a-jaw-bu-ŋar/ 'voyager (one who goes on the road)' in (33) shows the interaction of Extraprosodicity, Structure Preservation and Stray Erasure. The single morphemes <u>jaw</u> 'go' and <u>ŋar</u> 'road' are the inputs to the first cycle. The segments are syllabified according to the template, and the final consonant is defined extraprosodic.

(33) Lexical Derivation:

   1st cycle

Syllabification/Ex.

Stray Erasure: inapplicable

On the next cycle, a 'person marker' and bu 'noun marker (class 9)' are prefixed.

(34)
    2nd cycle

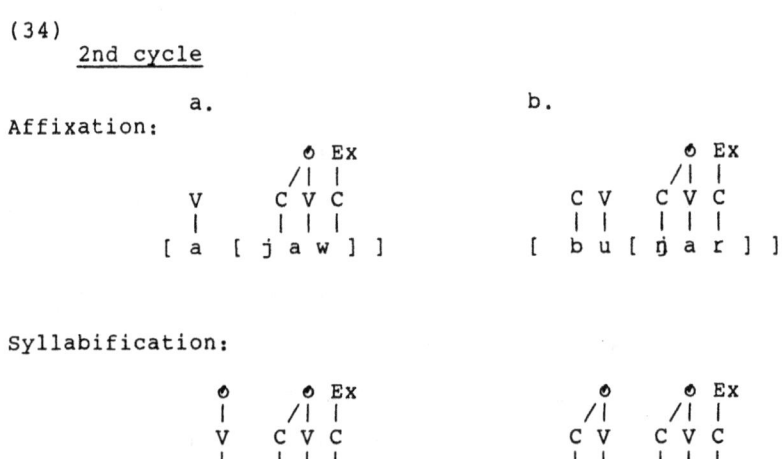

Stray Erasure: inapplicable

Since all the segments are licensed at this stage either by syllabification or by extraprosodicity, Stray Erasure does not takes place.

After Compounding (35) the final segments of the two compound members have a very different fate. The final w of the first compound member ajaw is now in an internal position and loses its extraprosodicity. Since it cannot be syllabified as a coda because of Structure Preservation, it is deleted by Stray Erasure.

(35)
   3rd cycle

Compounding:

Syllab.   blocked by SP

Stray
Erasure:

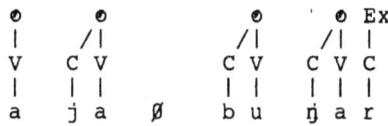

On the other hand, the final r of the second compound member is still extraprosodic at this stage of the derivation and is therefore not erased. Postlexically it loses its extraprosodic status, but since Structure Preservation no longer holds, it can be incorporated into the final syllable. This is shown in (36).

(36) Postlexical Derivation

Syll.

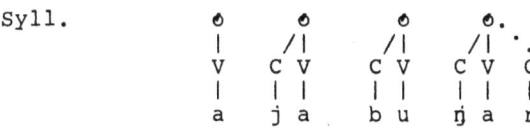

Stray Erasure: inapplicable

3.1.5 The Ordering versus the Continuous Hypothesis

In the Ordering Theory of Syllabification, it is argued that by arranging syllable-building rules and phonological rules appropriately in the derivation, the desired surface syllabification can be achieved. The Diola Coda Rule (37) (Steriade (1982:285) adjoins a consonant as a coda if it is segmentally linked to the following consonant and the following consonant is in the word template.[5] The restriction on the rule is referred to as 'the segmental linking condition.'

(37) Diola Fogny Coda Rule

$$\begin{array}{c} R. \\ / \quad \cdot \cdot \\ V \quad \cdot C_1 \quad C_2 \end{array}$$

If C_1 is segmentally linked to a following C_2 and C_2 is in the word template.

The segmental linking condition provides the key to the ordering of syllabification rules. The Coda Rule (37) must be ordered after Nasal Assimilation which creates the crucial segmental link. Since the Core Syllable Rule

---

[5]The original formulation includes [+son] in the structural description. It has been modified here because all consonants are segmentally linked, as discussed in 3.1.2 above.

universally applies first in the cycle, we have the following ordering of rules.

(38)
    Onset Rule (= Core syllable rule)
    (
    Nasal Assimilation (Melody Spread)
    (
    Coda Rule (37)

Although the theoretical assumptions seem very different, namely continuous and automatic syllabification vs. ordered once-a-cycle syllabification, the derivational history of the forms involving Nasal Assimilation is identical:[6] Nasal Assimilation precedes Coda syllabification (see the derivation in (29)). In the Ordering Theory, the Coda Rule (37) applies after Nasal Assimilation because the rules are ordered in this way. In the Continuous Syllabification Theory proposed here, codas are syllabified as soon as and whenever this is permitted by the Coda Condition (18), a situation which arises only after Assimilation in this particular case. Let us then compare these two theories. The Ordering Theory assumes noncontinuous once-a-cycle syllabification, resulting in a more powerful theory which allows for many unnatural extrinsic orderings of syllabification rules. For example,

---

[6]This is also pointed out by Steriade (1982) for a similar case in Attic Greek.

the rules in (38) could be ordered so that Nasal
Assimilation follows the Coda Rule (37).

(39)
    Onset Rule (= Core syllable rule)
    (
    Coda Rule (37)
    (
    Nasal Assimilation (Melody Spread)

With this ordering, an assimilated nasal cannot be syllabified on the cycle and is a potential target for Stray Erasure. It is rather doubtful whether such cases exist, at least I have not encountered any examples of this kind in my work. If they do not exist, it seems clear that extrinsic ordering is the wrong mechanism to ensure that assimilation applies before coda syllabification in Diola. Under the more restrictive Continuous Syllabification Theory, the situation characterized in (39) can never arise.

    Further arguments can be brought to bear against the Coda Rule (37) which carries the descriptive burden in the Ordering Theory. As discussed in chapter 2, a Coda Rule which stipulates segmental linking must explicitly look into the next syllable, violating the principle of Locality. On the other hand, the Coda Condition (18) needs no such stipulation, because the exhaustive linking interpretation of structural descriptions is universal.

Thus while accounting for the same facts in a very similar way, the Continuous Syllabification Hypothesis is more restrictive, less stipulative and maintains the principle of Locality.

3.1.6 Triconsonantal cluster simplification

Let us now return to the paradigm of cluster simplification in Diola. We still have to account for the fact that the first <u>two</u> consonants delete in a triconsonantal cluster, as shown by the examples in (7) (repeated below in (40)).

(40)
/e-rent-rent/ --> ererent   'it is light'
/na-maɲj-maɲj/ --> namamaɲj   'he knows'

Recall that in Kiparsky's (1973) analysis these cases involved a problematic disjunction in the consonant deletion rule (see (9) above). In our analysis, the elision of two consonants is the result of medial Stray Erasure triggering desyllabification which in turn triggers another application of Stray Erasure. This interaction is an automatic consequence of the theory for the cases at hand and not the result of ordering stipulations.

After Melody Spread, the examples in (40) have the structures shown in (41).

(41)
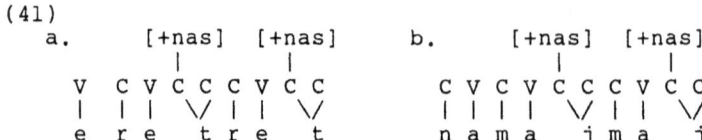

Since the two examples have identical derivations in all essential respects, I will limit my discussion to (41a). Here syllabification yields the following structure:

(42)
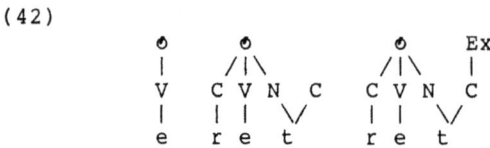

The final C is extraprosodic, and the final syllable is wellformed because its coda nasal is linked to the extraprosodic C. The medial skeletal C slot cannot be syllabified: The syllable template of Diola is CVVC and Structure Preservation will not allow the medial t in [eren̯trent] to be syllabified either as a coda (43a) or as an onset (43b).

(43)
a.
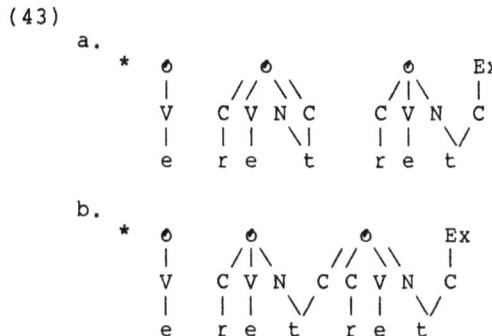

b.

The syllable structures *CVCC and *CCVC both violate Structure Preservation. The medial C remains therefore unsyllabified and is stray-erased to fulfill Prosodic Licensing as shown in (44).

(44)
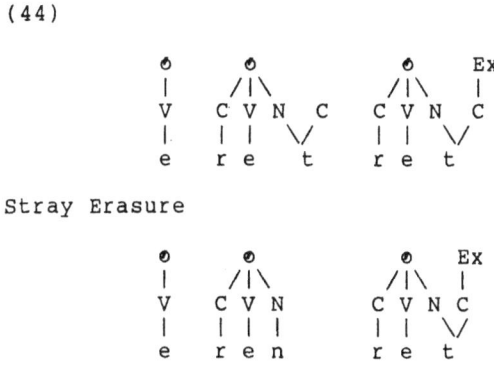

Stray Erasure

Now all segments are prosodically licensed, but Structure Preservation is violated. Once the medial skeletal C is erased, the coda consonant of the medial syllable is no longer protected by the double link and becomes fully exposed to the Coda Condition. The situation is automatically remedied by desyllabification of the offending segment.[7]

(45)

Now Prosodic Licensing is again no longer fulfilled and Stray Erasure must takes place, deleting the skeletal slot as well as the melody.[8]

---

[7]Notice that this is not a special desyllabification rule. Lexical structure simply does not tolerate any deviance from lexical constraints.

[8]The case of /-manj-manj/ --> -mamanj is revealing in another respect. The question is why we do not get -mammanj. After the medial j is stray-erased -manmanj we might expect Nasal Assimilation to apply yielding -mammanj. (This is not expected for erenrent because nasals do not assimilate to liquids which are higher in sonority, see (27).) The medial nasal, being a doubly-linked geminate m, should then be syllabifiable. This shows that Melody Spread is not an 'anywhere rule', applying as soon as the structural description is met, but a regular phonological rule which applies only once-a-cycle. Stray Erasure, on the other hand, applies to a form and eliminates all unlicensed material before it enters a new cycle. There is no restriction on how many times Stray Erasure can apply. Just as syllabification, it applies as many times as necessary to provide a fully licensed phonological string.

(46)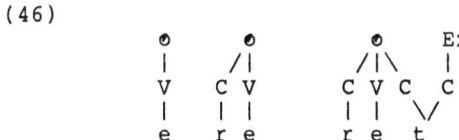

The Ordering Theory can deal with these cases because of the second part of the segmental linking condition on the Coda Rule (37), where reference is made to the word template specified to contain an initial and a final optional extrametrical C position (Steriade 1982:284).

(47) Diola Fogny Word Template : [(C) σ* (C)]

Being in the word template means either being syllabified or being a word-edge consonant.[9]

The word template (47) comes crucially into play in the triconsonantal case. After the Onset Rule and Melody Spread have applied, the Coda Rule can only apply to the final syllable, because the medial nasal consonant, although segmentally linked, is linked to a C-slot which is not in the word template, i.e. neither syllabified nor at the word-edge.

---

[9]It is perhaps of some interest that a syllabification rule is here conditioned by a template which is itself defined in terms of syllables.

(48)
a. Onset Rule --
   Spread

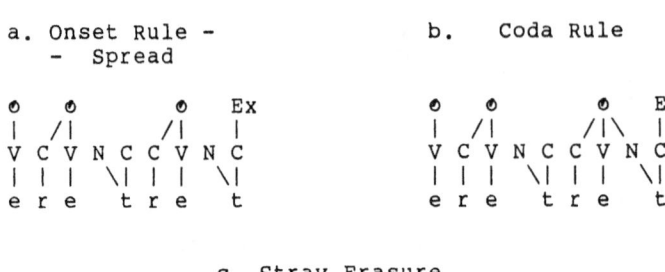

b. Coda Rule

c. Stray Erasure

The Coda Rule (37) cannot apply to the medial skeletal slot, and two consonants are correctly deleted word-medially by Stray Erasure.

The derivation of <u>ererent</u> under the Ordering Theory in (48) is simpler than that in (44-46) since it does not go through a stage where the medial [n] is syllabified. This is a spurious advantage over the Continuous Syllabification Theory, however, given the fact that it is achieved by crucial reference to the word template in the Coda Rule. Derivational simplicity is gained at the cost of another stipulation.

Suppose the reference to the word template were dropped. A separate desyllabification rule would then be needed to undo the Coda Rule when the structural description of the Coda Rule is no longer met. To adopt a desyllabification approach would be undesirable because desyllabification would also have to be a separate rule ordered in the phonology. Note that genuine phonological rules are usually not undone when their structural descriptions are no longer met.

In the Continuous Syllabification Theory, the derivation itself involves several steps and is more complex than in the Ordering Theory, but no stipulative reference to the word template is needed, and the principles which define the mechanisms are simple and derive from Universal Grammar. We can appeal to Structure Preservation and Prosodic Licensing and allow the actual syllabification as well as the desyllabification mechanisms to be completely free of extrinsic ordering and language-specific stipulations. As is usually the case, simplicity of principles entails derivational complexity.

3.2 Lardil Word Final Truncations

Lardil, an Australian language spoken on Mornington Island in the Gulf of Carpentaria, is analyzed by Hale (1973) and Klokeid (1976) in a segmental framework. Wilkinson (1986) proposes a syllable-based analysis of various aspects of Lardil Phonology. Of interest to us here are the set of word-final truncations, which Wilkinson (1986) convincingly argues to be results of Stray Erasure.

In our terms, the analysis of Lardil consonant loss turns out to be remarkably similar to the Diola case. The difference in applicability of Stray Erasure will be attributed to a different setting of the word-level Extraprosodicity parameter.

3.2.1 Facts

Hale (1973) proposes three deletion rules which apply word-finally. The examples below, which are all uninflected forms, illustrate the application of each of these rules. (Capital letters indicate retroflexion.)

(49)
Final Vowel Deletion (FVD):   V --> ∅ / __#
    yalulu   -> yalul   'flame'   (cf. nonfuture yalulu-n)
    mayara   -> mayar   'rainbow' (cf. nonfuture mayara-n)
    kamputa -> kamput   'pandoanas nuts'

(50)
Consonant Cluster Reduction (CCR):   C --> ∅ / C __#
    Tant^{y}irk -> Tant^{y}ir   'hip'   (cf. Tant^{y}irk-in)
    waŋalk   -> waŋal   'boomerang' (cf. waŋalk-in)

(51)

Non-Coronal Deletion[10] (NCD):   C   --> ∅ / __#
                                [-cor]

   ŋaluk -> ŋalu   'story'   (cf. ŋaluk-in)

   peReŋ -> peRe   'vagina'   (cf. peReŋ-in)

Examples illustrating the application of both Final Vowel Deletion and Consonant Cluster Reduction are given in (52); of Final Vowel Deletion and Noncoronal Deletion in (53); and of all three rules in (54).

(52)   FVD   CCR

   yukarpa   --> yukarp   --> yukar   'husband'

   kantukantu --> kantukant --> kantukan   'red'

   wulunka   --> wulunk   --> wulun   'fruit sp.'

   wuTalt^{y}i   --> wuTalt^y --> wuTal   'meat'

(53)   FVD   NCD

   puTuka   --> puTuk   --> puTu   'short'

   ŋawuŋawu   --> ŋawuŋaw   --> ŋawuŋa   'termite'

   murkunima --> murkunim --> murkuni   'nullah'

---

[10]Hale (1973) formulates the rule as Nonapical Deletion, using the feature [+distributed]. This singles out noncoronal consonants and coronal distributed (lamino-alveolar) consonants. See discussion in section 3.2.2.

(54)   FVD   CCR   NCD

muŋkumuŋku -> muŋkumuŋk -> muŋkumuŋ -> muŋkumu
                                                                    'wooden axe'

tʸumputʸumpu -> tʸumputʸump -> tʸumputʸum -> tʸumputʸu
                                                                    'dragonfly'

3.2.2 Lardil syllable structure

As Wilkinson (1986) amply demonstrates, Consonant Cluster Reduction and Noncoronal Deletion are no longer necessary in a syllable-based analysis because they can be analyzed as instances of Stray Erasure.

In Lardil, codas come in two basic varieties: They can be coronals (55) or nasals (56).

(55)
    kar.mu   'bone'
    kan.tu   'blood'
    pir.ŋen   'woman'
    Rel.ka   'head'
    yaR.put   'snake, bird'
    wa.ŋal   'boomerang'

wu.luṉ   'fruit sp.'

ma.yar̠   'rainbow'

(56)

kuṇ̇.ka   'groin'

taṇ̇.ku   'oysters found in reefs'

ṅam.pit   'humpy'

kum.pu   'anus'

The segments ṇ̇ and m in coda position are subject to the restriction that the following syllable must start with a homorganic obstruent (k for ṇ̇ and p for m). There are no word-final noncoronal nasals. If we assume, as in the case of Diola, that there is a separate manner or nasal tier, homorganic nasal+obstruent clusters receive the representations in (57).

(57)

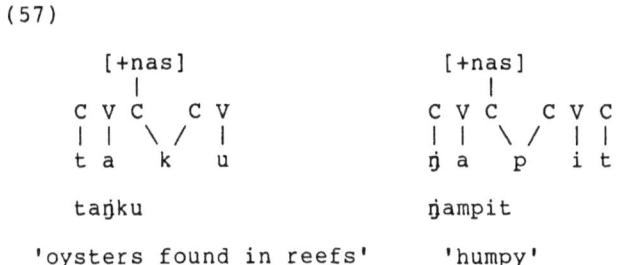

taŋku   ṅampit
'oysters found in reefs'   'humpy'

The Lardil syllable analysis (reinterpreted from Wilkinson's (1986) syllable-building rule approach into

(58) Lardil Syllable Analysis:

    a.   CV-Template: [C V V C]

    b.   Coda Condition: * C]$_\sigma$
                                                   |
                                                 [-cor]

The Lardil Coda Condition (58b) prohibits syllable-final noncoronals. Being [+coronal], the segment <u>l</u> in (59a) can be syllabified, and being doubly-linked, the segment <u>m</u> in (59b) can become a coda.

(59)

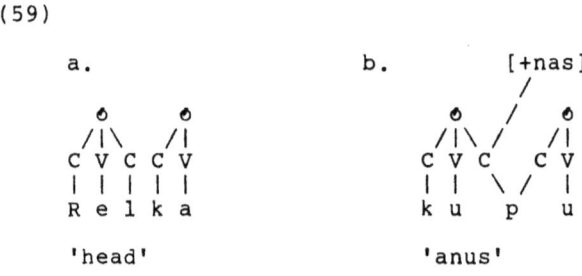

    'head'   'anus'

The Coda Condition given in (58b) does not quite account for all the cases in Lardil. Apical and nonapical coronals differ in that only the former are allowed to be syllabified as codas. Relating this fact to certain dissimilation rules in Lardil, Wilkinson (1986), following Stevens et. al. (1986), captures the apical/nonapical contrast by means of the feature [back] and proposes to restrict the Coda Rule to nonback (i.e. apical) coronals.

(60)   Lardil Coda Rule (Wilkinson 1986)

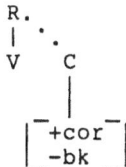

The restriction incorporated into this rule involves a conjunction of two features and can therefore not be expressed without a disjunction in terms of a <u>negative</u> Coda Condition. This is not a problem, since we can formulate an equivalent and disjunctionless <u>positive</u> condition (61) (see section 2.4 of chapter 2 for the formal equivalence of positive and negative conditions).

(61) Lardil Coda Condition (revised)

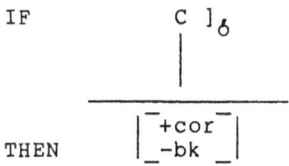

For ease of exposition, I will continue to refer only to the coronal/noncoronal distinction.

As a brief illustration consider the examples in (62).

(62)

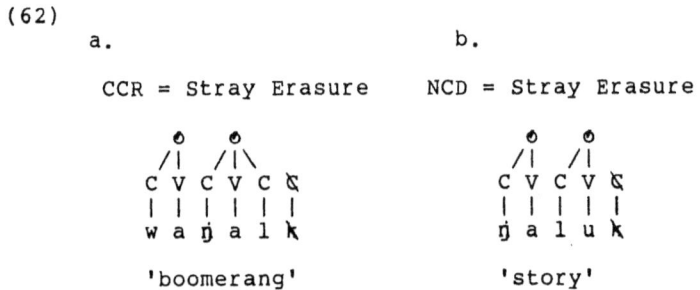

    a. CCR = Stray Erasure   b. NCD = Stray Erasure

    w a ṅ a l k   ṅ a l u k

    'boomerang'   'story'

The final k in waṅalk (62a) is not part of any syllable, because no space is left in the template of the preceding syllable. In ṅaluk (62b), the final k cannot be a syllable-final consonant because of (61). Both k's are thus subject to Stray Erasure.

3.2.3 Word-level Phonology

I will assume that Apocope is a word-level deletion rule.[11]

(63) Apocope: V --> ∅ / ____]

It is not necessary to stipulate that this rule applies only at the word level because the Strict Cycle blocks its application at earlier levels (see Kiparsky 1983 for similar cases). That Apocope is a word-level phenomenon is confirmed by the fact that it is blocked by the Minimal Word Requirement (64) requiring words to be at least two moras long.

(64) Lardil Minimal Word Requirement (Wilkinson 1986)

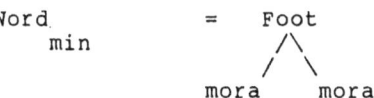

Thus the bimoraic words in (65) do not undergo Apocope.

---

[11]Wilkinson (1986) proposes to deal with this also as a case of Stray Erasure by making two additional assumption: (i) final vowels are extrametrical, and (ii) extrametrical vowels are subject to Stray Erasure.

(65)

/kela/	-->	kela, *kel	'beach'
/mela/	-->	mela, *mel	'sea'
/ŋuku/	-->	nuka, *ŋuk, *nu	'water'
/papi/	-->	pape, *pap, *pa	'father's mother'

The last two forms in (65) show Final Vowel Lowering, which only applies to stem-final vowels. I will assume, following Hale (1973), that Apocope is ordered after Final Vowel Lowering so that only the underlyingly stem-final vowels are lowered.[12]

At the word level, the Strict Cycle no longer holds, but Structure Preservation is still enforced. Therefore syllable structures that do not conform to the lexical syllable requirements in (58) cannot be built.

The word-level derivations for (i) <u>yalulu</u> 'flame,' (ii) <u>puTuka</u> 'short,' and (iii) <u>nuku</u> 'water' are given in (66). Each derivational step is explained below.

---

[12]In order to satisfy the <u>minimum word requirement</u>, there is also an augmentation rule which supplies /a/ to an unsuffixed monomoraic stem.

(i) /wik/ --> wika   'shade'
    /yur/ --> yura   'body'

(66)

Word level

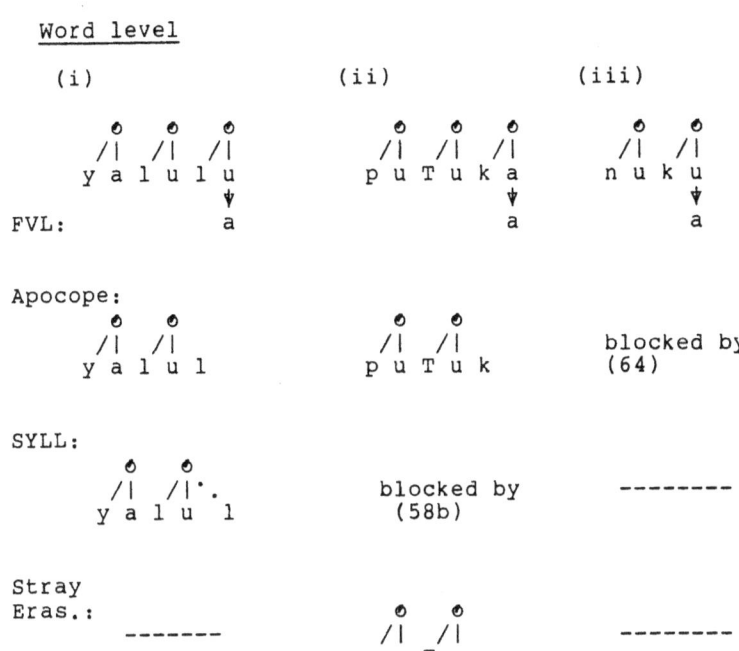

- All three forms enter the word level fully syllabified.

- Final Vowel Lowering applies to all three forms, (vacuously for puTuka).

- Apocope is blocked in (iii) because of the Minimal Word Requirement (64). It applies in (i) and (ii), yielding yalul and puTuk. I assume that the final syllable node disappears together with the syllabic nucleus, which is an obligatory part of the syllable.

- The final consonants in (i) and (ii) are now syllabically unaffiliated. Syllabification can incorporate the coronal l in (i) but not the noncoronal k in (ii) because of the Coda Condition (61).

- Stray Erasure then eliminates the unlicensed k in (ii).

Let us now turn to more complex cases like /muŋkumuŋku/ --> muŋkumu and /yukarpa/ --> yukar. Here representations with skeleton are necessary. The nasal tier is encoded as N on the skeleton.

The string is syllabified as in (67). After Apocope, the final C cannot be syllabified, and the skeletal slot is deleted by Stray Erasure. Now the final noncoronal consonant in (i) is no longer doubly-linked and is therefore exposed to the Coda Condition. Structure Preservation requires that the final consonant be desyllabified, making it susceptible to Stray Erasure.

(67)

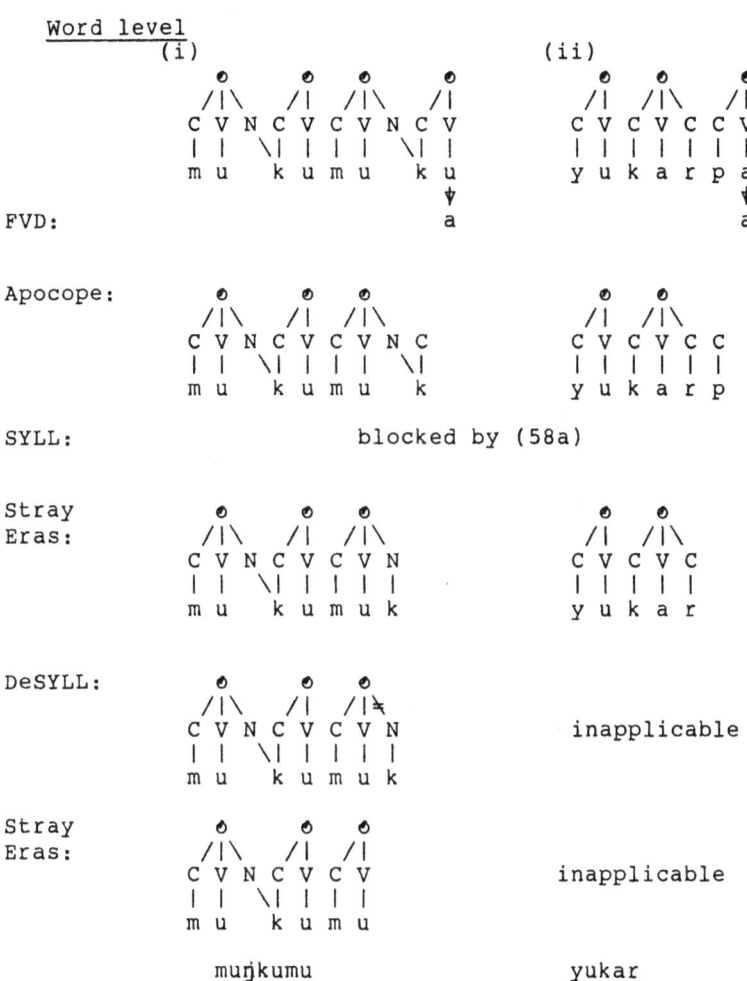

Underlying /t^yumput^yumpu/ goes through the same kind of derivation: The final [u] is deleted by Apocope, [p] is stray-erased, [m] is desyllabified and also stray-erased, resulting in t^yumput^yu.

One consequence of our theory is that the members of final clusters are erased individually by separate applications of Stray Erasure, with Desyllabification intervening. An analysis in which final clusters are deleted en bloc by a single application of Stray Erasure (or some deletion rule) makes wrong predictions for forms with coronal clusters as in (68).

(68)   Apocope

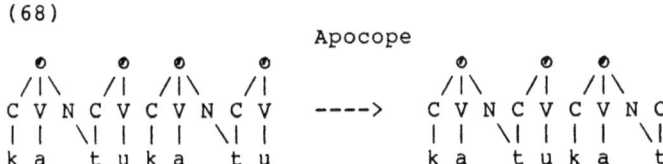

The structure after Apocope is identical to that given for muŋkumuŋk in (67). Consider the output after the first application of Stray Erasure:

(69)   Stray Erasure

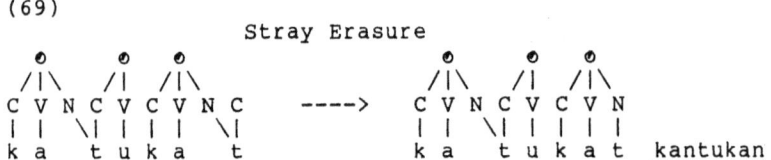

kantukan

The final syllable is wellformed because it ends in a coronal consonant and therefore does not undergo desyllabification. This is independent support for the Stray Erasure/Desyllabification analysis given here. An analysis which eliminates the entire final cluster would not be able to distinguish between the coronal cluster and the noncoronal cluster and yield muŋkumu as well as the ungrammatical *kantuka.

An interesting idea pursued in Wilkinson's (1986) rule-based analysis is that of nondistinctness. The Coda Rule (60) cannot straightforwardly deal with nasal noncoronals homorganic to the following consonant. The nondistinctness analysis assumes that the homorganic nasals are nasal archisegments unspecified for place of articulation features in the phonology and that the Coda Rule applies to segments which are nondistinct from [+coronal]. This solution is superior to a segmental linking condition since it does not violate Locality in requiring syllable-external information. The assumption behind this nondistinctness analysis is that these nasals are unspecified for place when the syllable-building rules apply. When the coda is later specified as noncoronal by assimilation, it no longer has to meet the structural description of the Coda Rule (60) since the syllable-building rules have already applied.

The nondistinctness analysis encounters a problem in the cases where two homorganic consonants are lost in final position, as in /muŋkumuŋku/ --> muŋkumu and

/tʸumputʸumpu/ --> tʸumputʸu 'dragonfly'. In these examples, the Coda Rule applies to all the unspecified nasals.

(70)

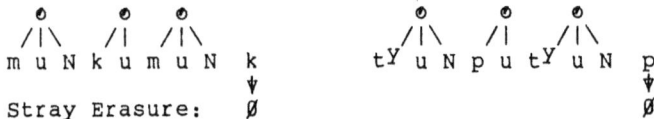

The problem is that the deletion of the final nasal in these examples cannot be attributed to Stray Erasure, which applies to the final consonant but not to the (syllabified) unspecified N.[13]

As shown in the derivation in (67), the analysis proposed here can deal with these cases in a very natural way. Stating the language-specific properties of codas as a wellformedness condition, with free syllabification and desyllabification applying continuously throughout the derivation, allows us to express the generalization

---

[13]One possibility in the nondistinctness analysis (suggested to me by John McCarthy) is to recognize two types of Stray Erasure: Stray -unsyllabified- Erasure and Stray -unspecified- Erasure. Assuming that Stray -unsyllabified- Erasure applies before assimilation, Stray -unspecified- Erasure applies only to the word-final nasals which fail to receive any specification after assimilation. This would delete only the word-final nasal archisegments which are not in an assimilation environment. But note that it must then be assumed that the nasals in kantukan are not archisegments but rather specified for coronality.

about the Lardil coda as a single statement. No other
statements in the grammar duplicate this information.

3.2.4 Word-Level Extraprosodicity: Comparison with Diola

In both Lardil and Diola, Stray Erasure of
unsyllabified consonants plays a prominent role. In the
analysis of Diola (see section 3.1), final consonants are
licensed as extraprosodic and are therefore not subject
to Stray Erasure. It seems natural to assume that the
difference between Lardil and Diola lies in the setting
of the Extraprosodicity parameter.

Let us now investigate in which ways Extraprosodicity
can be language-specific. It is clearly not the case that
Extraprosodicity is totally absent from Lardil phonology.
For example, Lardil also needs to assume that final
consonants are extraprosodic during the lexical cycles,
so that edge segments can be saved by affixation. The
alternations found between the unaffixed and affixed forms
(ṅalu vs. ṅaluk-in 'story-nonfuture') are revealing in this
respect. On the first cycle [ṅaluk], the final consonant
k cannot be syllabified because of Structure Preservation.
But Stray Erasure must not apply to k, because it surfaces
in the suffixed form [[ṅaluk]in]. Cases such as these
are the basis for the claim by earlier researchers that

Stray Erasure does not apply until later in the derivation. This is not a necessary conclusion, however. We can distinguish between lexical Extraprosodicity and word-level Extraprosodicity. Lexical Extraprosodicity is universal and defines edge segments as extraprosodic throughout the lexical derivation before the word level. Word-level Extraprosodicity, on the other hand, is stipulated on a language-particular basis. In the case of Lardil, there is no extraprosodic licensing at the word level. The cyclic derivation of the affixed ṇaluk-in and the unaffixed ṇalu is given in (71).

(71)

Lexical level:

1 cycle

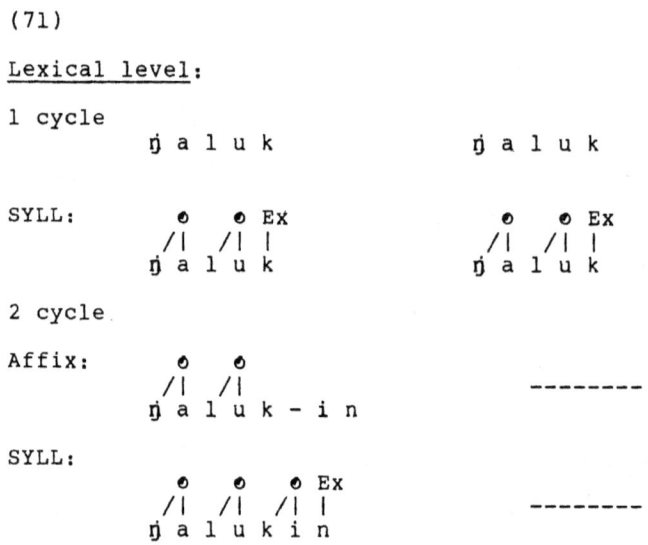

(71cont.)
Word level:

```
         σ   σ   σ                           σ   σ
        /|  /|  /|                          /|  /|
        ŋ a l u k i n                       ŋ a l u k
```

SYLL:
```
         σ   σ    σ
        /|  /|\  /|\                       blocked by
        w a ŋ a l k i n                    Structure Preserv.
```

Stray
Eras: inapplicable
```
                                            σ   σ
                                           /|  /|\
                                           w a ŋ a l ∅
```

Since Structure Preservation still holds at the word level, syllables violating the lexical constraints cannot be formed. Stray Erasure eliminates all unlicensed material before the string enters the postlexical level. In Diola, on the other hand, the language-specific option of word-level Extraprosodicity is invoked, and it is only at the postlexical level, where Extraprosodicity is universally absent that all segments must be syllabically licensed. However, since Structure Preservation no longer holds postlexically, syllabification can adjoin segments to the edge syllable without having to respect lexical syllable constraints. Thus final extraprosodicity at the word level allows word-edge syllables in Diola to be superheavy and to disregard the Coda Condition.

The paradigm below summarizes our assumptions about

extraprosodicity and the types of parametric variation:

(72) Extraprosodicity

Lexical	-	universal	on
Word Level	-	language-specific	on/[off]
Postlexical	-	universal	off

The unmarked case for word-level Extraprosodicity is assumed to be off (i.e. the Lardil case). Since word-level Extraprosodicity is language-specific, it can be further marked as involving not just a final segment but a particular kind of segment. For example, in Attic Greek the word-level final-extraprosodic segment is specified as s (Steriade 1982). Lexical Extraprosodicity, being universal, cannot be restricted to a particular type of segment. This has important consequences, as we will see in the next section.

3.3 Attic Greek Consonant Loss

The basis for this section is the analysis of Attic Greek prosody in Steriade (1982).[14] The syllable condition to be proposed for Attic Greek has a more complex structure since laryngeal linking plays a crucial role.

3.3.1 Attic Greek syllable structure

In Attic Greek, a syllable can be closed by sonorant consonants and by the continuant s.[15] (The lax mid vowels of Attic Greek are represented as ę and ǫ.)

(73) a̲r.no̲s   'lamb'
      a̲s.tʰma   'panting'
      gin̲.glu.mo̲s   'hinge'
      a̲r.tʰmo̲s   'bond'
      pʰa̲s.ga.no̲n   'sword'
      pū̲r   'fire'

---

[14] I would like to note here that the analysis of Attic Greek syllabification in Steriade (1982) first started my thinking about the segmental linking condition in syllable structure and its relationship to the Geminate Constraint in general.

[15] For an analysis of the possible types of onsets, see Steriade (1982).

Noncontinuant obstruents, on the other hand, are in certain circumstances lost in coda position. This is shown word-finally in (74) and word-internally in (75).

(74)
    a. /meli<u>t</u>/ --> meli 'honey-VOC'
    b. /gunai<u>k</u>/ --> gunai 'woman-VOC'
    c. /damar<u>t</u>/ --> damar 'spouse-VOC'
    d. /gala<u>kt</u>/ --> gala 'milk-VOC'

(75)
    a. /pe-pē<u>t</u>ʰ-<u>k</u>-a/ --> pepēka 'I have persuaded'
    b. /p̃nu<u>t</u>-<u>k</u>-a/ --> p̃nuka 'I have accomplished'
    c. /ke-komi<u>d</u>-<u>k</u>-a/ --> kekomika 'I have provided'

Coda plosives are allowed if part of a geminate as in (76).

(76)
    pa<u>p.p</u>os 'grandfather'
    pra<u>t.t</u>ō 'to do'
    ba<u>k.k</u>ʰos 'name of deity'

The data considered so far can be accounted for by the following coda condition:

(77) Attic Greek Coda Condition

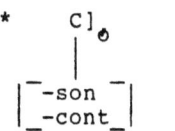

Coda syllabification takes place in (78) and in (80) but not in (79) where I assume, with Steriade (1982), that the unsyllabifiable consonants are deleted by Stray Erasure.

(78)
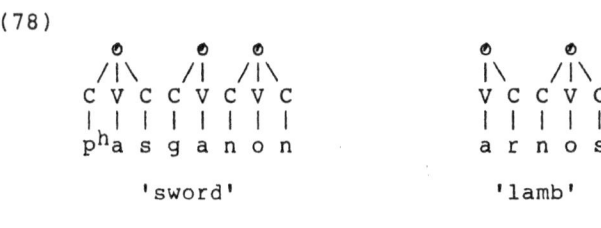

'sword'   'lamb'

(79)

'honey-VOC'   'I have provided'

(80)
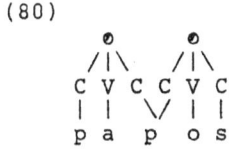   

'grandfather'   'name of deity'

As formulated in (77), however, the Attic Greek Coda Condition rules out too much. For example, a coda obstruent is allowed if the adjacent consonant (i.e. the onset of the following syllable) is a coronal obstruent.

(81)

ok.tō   'eight'
a.elp.tos   'unhoped for'
e.derkʰ.tʰēn   'I was seen'
ekʰ.tʰros   'hateful'
ʰeb.do.mas   'week'

Word-finally, plosive consonants are retained if they precede final s as in (82). (These cases should be compared with examples like /galakt/ --> gala (74), in which final obstruents are deleted.)

(82)

pʰleps   'vein'
tʰōrāks   'chest'

Since the forms in (81) and (82) do not have a doubly-linked melody, the structural description of the Coda Condition (77) is met, and we incorrectly predict that the consonants in these positions are unsyllabifiable and hence deleted by Stray Erasure.

The interesting solution proposed in Steriade (1982) relies on the fact that these forms have doubly-linked laryngeal features arising through the application of various independently motivated laryngeal-tier rules.[16] (Notice that the relevant coda consonant and the following onset consonant in (81) and (82) share voicing and aspiration features.) For example, Laryngeal Feature Assimilation (LFA) <u>spreads the laryngeal features of a coronal to the preceding obstruent</u> so that sequences such as <u>kd</u>, <u>bs</u>, <u>kt^h</u> become <u>gd</u>, <u>ps</u>, <u>k^{h}t^h</u>, respectively. The application of LFA is illustrated in (83), where /leg-t^{h}ɛ̄somai/ becomes /lek^h-t^{h}ɛ̄somai/.

(83)

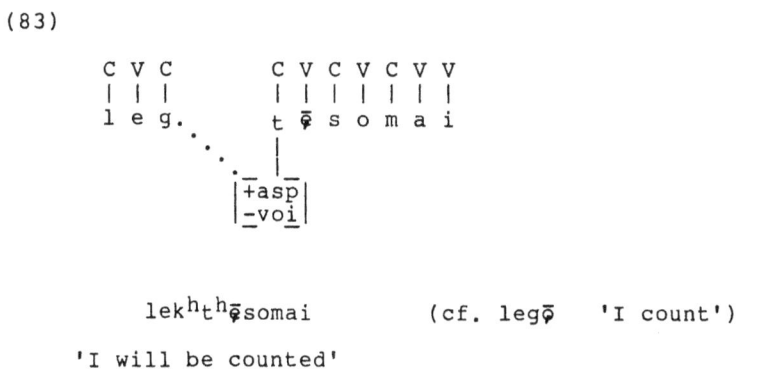

    lek^{h}t^{h}ɛ̄somai   (cf. legɔ̄   'I count')

'I will be counted'

---

[16]For extensive justification for the laryngeal rules, see Steriade (1982).

Assuming with Steriade (1982) that such laryngeal links are responsible for coda syllabification, I propose to revise the Attic Coda Condition as follows.[17]

(84) Attic Greek Coda Condition (revised)

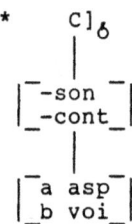

The association line to the laryngeal tier is now part of the structural description. If there is a double link either from the core melody tier as in (85a) or from the

---

[17]Instead of a syllable structure condition, we might express this as a sequential melody constraint of the type discussed for Finnish in chapter 2, section 2.6. The generalization for Attic Greek is that obstruent sequences are allowed only when the second obstruent is a coronal.

(i)

　　　* [-son]　$\begin{bmatrix} -cor \\ -son \end{bmatrix}$

This sequential constraint disallows *kp, *pk, *tk, *tp but allows kt, pt, bd, as well as [-son][+son] sequences. Under the current conception of nonlinear phonology, however, there is no direct way of deriving the actual consonant loss from a sequential constraint.

laryngeal tier as in (85b), syllabification of the relevant consonants as codas is not prohibited.[18]

(85)
    a.   b.

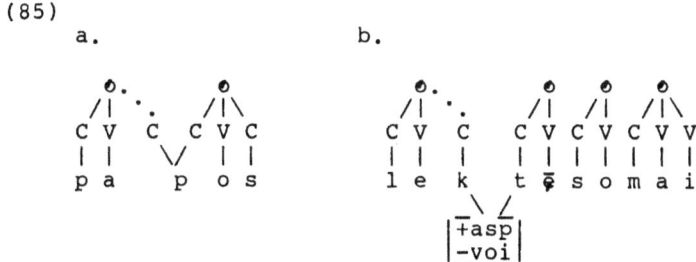

The revised Coda Condition (84) is intended to replace the following Attic Greek Coda Rule.

(86) Attic Greek Coda Rule   (Steriade 1982:225)

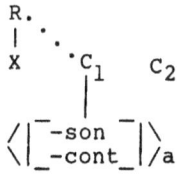

                                                  $<C_1$ is segmentally linked to C_2 and C_2 is in the word template.$>_b$
                                                  a only if b

(87)   Attic Greek Word Template : [(C) σ* (s)]$_w$

---

[18] For recent views on further separation of tiers in the autosegmental framework, see Clements (1985), McCarthy (1985), Mester (1986), Steriade and Schein (to appear).

The Coda Rule applies to [+son] and to [+cont] consonants without restriction. The part of the rule in angled brackets ensures that plosives are syllabified as codas only when they are segmentally linked to a following consonant that is in the word template (87).

The important parts of the word template for Attic Greek (87) can be recast in our framework as word-level Extraprosodicity of an initial consonant and a final s̲. The fact that words consists internally of a sequence of syllables does not need to be stated in a language-specific template since this is given universally by the Principle of Prosodic Licensing.

I will briefly illustrate how the assumption that word-level Extraprosodicity is restricted to s̲ accounts for the various types of consonant loss as well as the unexpected types of consonant retention.

An example of word-internal consonant loss is seen in /ke-komid-ka/ --> kekomika (75c). On the first cycle [komid] the final consonant d̲ is extraprosodic. By the affixation of -ka, the d̲, no longer being final, loses its extraprosodic status. Structure Preservation prohibiting coda syllabification of an obstruent, Stray Erasure takes place at the end of the cycle.

On the first cycle of /gunaik/ 'woman' (74b), the final consonant is extraprosodic, and it appears in the surface form when vowel-initial suffixes are added, as

in gunaik-i 'woman dat.' If the form enters the word level
unaffixed or with a Ø-affix, the final consonant is no
longer extraprosodic because the language-specific
Extraprosodicity for Attic is restricted to final s.
Structure Preservation still holds at the word level, and
Prosodic Licensing requires the final k to be eliminated
by Stray Erasure (i.e. /gunaik/ --> gunai) in the vocative,
where the affix is Ø.

In deriving /pʰleb-s/, the final consonant b is
extraprosodic on the first cycle. When the nominative
-s is added, b loses its extraprosodic status, and the
final s is extraprosodic. Laryngeal Feature Assimilation
links the b with the final s (i.e. pʰleb-s --> pʰleps),
and coda syllabification is now allowed. At the word
level, the final s is again defined as extraprosodic, this
time by the language-specific provision. Postlexically,
Structure Preservation does not hold and the final s can
be adjoined to the syllable.

3.3.2 Word-Level Extraprosodicity and Stray Erasure

To summarize, Stray Erasure is seen to apply
word-medially during the lexical cycles, and word-finally
at the word level. At the postlexical level, the segments
which have survived through the word level can be

syllabified because Structure Preservation no longer holds.

In Diola, Stray Erasure has no chance to apply at the word level because language-specific extraprosodicity licenses all final consonants. In Lardil, on the other hand, there is no word-level Extraprosodicity, therefore all unsyllabifiable final consonants are subject to Stray Erasure. In Attic Greek, only s is licensed by word-level Extraprosodicity, and therefore other unsyllabifiable consonants are eliminated.[19] Because of the restricted nature of word-level Extraprosodicity in Attic Greek, it represents the hybrid situation.

Viewed in this way, the question 'Where does Stray Erasure apply in language x?' is no longer a valid one. It can universally apply at the end of every cycle to prosodically unlicensed segments. Differences arise as a result of the language-specific parameter of word-level Extraprosodicity. Other properties follow from the interaction of the universal principles motivated in Lexical Phonology and Prosodic Phonology.

---

[19]Initial Extraprosodicity in Attic Greek is more liberal then final Extraprosodicity, see Steriade (1982).

CHAPTER IV

SYLLABIFICATION AND STRAY OPERATIONS

4.0 **Introduction**

A common, if informal, observation is that languages employ either Stray Erasure or Stray Epenthesis to deal with material left over from syllabification. As shown in (1), Korean and Attic Greek[1] eliminate unsyllabified segments by Stray Erasure, while in parallel circumstances Chukchee and Cairene Arabic insert a vowel by Stray Epenthesis to save unsyllabified segments (2). Thus both Stray Erasure and Stray Epenthesis result in representations which no longer contain stray segments.

(1) **Stray Erasure:**

a. Korean
```
          σ
         /|\
/kaps/ --> kap s -->   kap         "price"

             σ    σ
            /|\  /|
/kaps-to/ --> kap s to  -->  kap t'o   "price-too"
```

---

[1]See section 3.3 for a discussion of Stray Erasure in Attic Greek.

(1cont.)

b.   Attic Greek

```
                    o  o
                   /|  /|
/galakt/  -->   ga la kt  -->  gala        "milk"


                     o o    o
                    /|/|    /|
/ke-komid-ka/ -->  komi d  ka -->  -komika    "I have provided"
```

(2)   Stray Epenthesis:

a.   Chukchee

```
                         o
                        /|\
/loŋl/   -->     loŋ l   -->   loŋ@l         "walrus fat - abs.sg"

                                          (@ = schwa)

                     o o     o
                    /|/|\   /|
/ga-qapl-ma/ -->  gaqap l  ma  ->  gaqapl@ma  "ball-comitative"
```

b.   Cairene

```
                       o o
                      /|/|\
/ma-katab-t-š/  -->  katab tš  -->  katabtiš
                                          "I/you didn't write"


                     o o    o
                    /|/|\  /|
/katab-t-l-u/ -->  katab t  lu  --> katabtilu
                                          "I/you wrote to him"
```

A single language may exhibit both Stray Epenthesis and Stray Erasure effects, depending on the nature of the stray segment. For example, Harris (1983) convincingly shows that the segments affected by Epenthesis and Erasure in Spanish are exactly those which cannot be incorporated into syllable structure (cf. also Harris 1969, 1977).

(3) <u>Stray Erasure and Stray Epenthesis</u> (Spanish)

a. $[-son] \rightarrow \emptyset \ / C \_\_ C$

    absor.<u>b</u>.to   -->   absorto   (cf. absor<u>b</u>er)
    escul.<u>p</u>.tor   -->   escultor   (cf. escul<u>p</u>ir)
    distin.<u>g</u>.to   -->   distinto   (cf. distin<u>g</u>ir)

b. $\emptyset \rightarrow e \ / \ \{{C \atop \#} \_\_ {rC \atop sC}\}$

    <u>s</u>.fera   -->   e<u>s</u>fera   (cf. hemi<u>s</u>ferio)
    <u>s</u>.lavo   -->   e<u>s</u>lavo   (cf. yugo<u>s</u>lavo)
    <u>s</u>.pirar   -->   e<u>s</u>pirar   (cf. in<u>s</u>pirar)
    frat.<u>r</u>.nal   -->   frate<u>r</u>nal   (cf. frat<u>r</u>icidio)
    lib.<u>r</u>.tador   -->   libe<u>r</u>tador (cf. lib<u>r</u>e)
    emped.<u>r</u>.nir   -->   empede<u>r</u>nir (cf. pied<u>r</u>a)

The [+cont] segments <u>s</u> and <u>r</u> are affected by Stray Epenthesis and are therefore not subject to Stray Erasure. Our general hypothesis is that both stray operations

bring the representations into conformity with Prosodic
Licensing at the end of each phonological cycle. Stray
Erasure is universal and always available as a last resort,
Stray Epenthesis, on the other hand, is subject to
parametric variation (the unmarked option [off] is
indicated by square brackets).

(4)

    Stray Erasure   ---   universal   on

    Stray Epenthesis --- parameterized   on/[off]

The marked option, if chosen, can be further restricted
by special conditions (e.g. limiting Stray Epenthesis to
more sonorous elements) and applies at the end of each
cycle before Stray Erasure.

Stray Erasure, although universal, has no visible
effects in cases where the syllable template is fairly
liberal or where Stray Epenthesis has applied to all stray
segments.

The term <u>stray epenthesis</u> is here used in a
descriptive way to refer to phenomena of the type given
in (2) and (3b). There are currently two competing views
on how to analyze this kind of epenthesis, the skeletal
rule approach and the syllable-mapping approach. The
former proposes to analyze stray epenthesis as a context

sensitive skeletal rule as given in (5), supplying a vowel to a stray consonant (indicated by C').

(5)
    a.   ∅ --> V /__ C'
    b.   ∅ --> V / C'__

The skeletal rule approach is in line with the Kahnian view of syllabification, essentially adopted in Steriade (1982) and Levin (1985), which takes syllabic segments (V-slots on the skeleton or nuclear X-slots) as starting points of syllable building. In this view, stray consonants cannot be incorporated into a syllable before vowel epenthesis since no syllable has yet been built into which they could be incorporated. As shown in (6), at least a V-slot must be supplied on the skeleton before syllable building can even start.

(6)

$$C' \rightarrow \begin{matrix} C' & V \\ | & \\ k & \end{matrix} \rightarrow \begin{matrix} & \sigma \\ & \cdot | \\ C & V \\ | & \\ k & \end{matrix}$$

In this view, insertion of the skeletal slot is a process entirely independent of the subsequent syllabification of the stray consonant. The melodic feature of the vocalic slot are supplied by default rules (Kiparsky 1982, Archangeli 1984).

In the syllable-mapping approach (proposed in Halle & Vergnaud 1978, Selkirk 1981, Lapointe & Feinstein 1982, etc.), it is hypothesized that epenthesis is an integral part of syllabification itself and consists in the assignment of minimal syllable structure to stray consonants as shown in (7).

(7) a.
```
                      σ
                     /|
         C'   -->   C V
         |          |
         t          t
```

b.
```
                      σ
                     |\
         C'   -->   V C
         |          |
         t          t
```

Epenthesis in the syllable-mapping approach can be stated in preliminary form as follows.

(8) Map stray consonant to syllable template.

Since the nuclear slot of a syllable is universally obligatory, the newly created syllable will always include an empty slot which is then filled in by default rules in the same way as in the skeletal approach.

The syllable-mapping theory of epenthesis presupposes the existence in the grammar of a syllable template to which elements can be associated. In a theory for which such prosodic structure only comes into existence through syllable-building rules of the Kahnian type proceeding in a bottom-up fashion, it is obviously not possible to assign syllables to stray elements in this way. The syllable-mapping approach to epenthesis is therefore only compatible with a templatic approach to syllabification like the one pursued in this dissertation, in which the syllable structure of a language is given in the form of a template and a set of language-specific wellformedness conditions.

In this chapter, I will compare the two theories of epenthesis with respect to epenthesis processes in Ponapean, Japanese and Axininca Campa, and I will show that the syllable-mapping theory avoids redundancies and is more desirable in various respects. In the course of the discussion, I will have occasion to consider some consequences of the Obligatory Contour Principle (Leben 1973, Goldsmith 1976, and more recently developed in McCarthy 1979b, 1981, 1986) and of Tier Conflation (Younes 1983, McCarthy 1986) for syllabification. The principles of Prosodic Phonology and Lexical Phonology discussed in chapter 3 will continue to play a key role.

4.1 Ponapean Epenthesis

The phonology and morphology of Ponapean (Rehg & Sohl 1981) relating to the highly complex system of reduplication found in this language have recently attracted much attention (McCarthy 1983, Levin 1985, McCarthy & Prince 1985). In this section, we will first compare the two approaches to stray epenthesis discussed in the introduction on the basis of the Ponapean data. We will then explore the relationship between epenthesis and assimilation rules as well as certain fusion processes accompanied by nasal substitution.

In Ponapean, biconsonantal clusters resulting from morpheme concatenation are broken up by an epenthetic vowel.[2]

(9) $C_1 C_2 \rightarrow C_1 V C_2$

a.	/kitik-men/	-->	kitik<u>i</u>men	'rat'
b.	/lus-san/	-->	lus<u>i</u>san	'jump from'
c.	/daur-di/	-->	daur<u>i</u>di	'climb downwards'
d.	/m^wesel-saŋ/	-->	m^wesel<u>i</u>saŋ	'leave from'
e.	/ak-p^wuŋ/	-->	ak<u>u</u>p^wuŋ	'petty'
f.	/ak-suwei/	-->	ak<u>u</u>suwei	'demonstrating boastfulness'

---

[2] Following Rehg and Sohl (1981), <u>t</u> represents retroflex affricates and <u>d</u> (voiceless) dental stops. Ponapean has no voiced obstruents.

In (9a) the epenthetic vowel i breaks up the cluster km. The epenthetic vowel is a high front vowel subject to backing in a [+back] environment (see e.g. (9e,f)).[3]

4.1.1 Ponapean syllable structure

Ponapean syllables are either open (10) or closed by the first segment of a geminate (11) or a consonant homorganic to the onset of the next syllable (12).

(10)
        pereki   'to order'

        sap^{w}ele   'to shovel'

        karasapene   'to compare'

        lusida   'to jump upwards'

        lapake   'flood'

---

[3] Depending on morpheme size and class, the inserted vowel can be a copy of the nearby base vowel, a floating stem vowel, or an epenthetic vowel. Only the latter is fully productive (see Rehg and Sohl (1981) for details).

(11)

arewalla	'to return to the wild'
rerrer	'to be trembling'
kemmad	'to change into dry clothing'
urenna	'lobster'
kamʷmʷus	'to cause to vomit'
kaŋŋet	'to cause to pant'
nappa	'Chinese cabbage' (loanword)
kakko	'putting on airs' (loanword)
kiassi	'catcher' (loanword)

(12)

nampar	'trade wind season'
naŋkep	'inlet'
dindil	'penetrate'

The occurrence of final consonant clusters (13) reveals the existence of word-level final Extraprosodicity. Notice that the final clusters are also homorganic (including geminates).

(13)

    lem^{w}m^w 'afraid of ghosts'

    mall   'clearing'

    mand   'tame'

    kens   'yaws'

    emp   'coconut crab'

There is independent evidence in the phonology of Ponapean for the extraprosodic status of final consonants. McCarthy (1983) points out that the pattern of Monosyllabic Noun Lengthening can be understood by final consonant extraprosodicity.[4] Consider the forms in (14).

(14)   Monosyllabic Noun Lengthening:

    pik --> piik   'sand'   (cf. pik-en)

    keep --> keep, *keeep 'yam'   (cf. keep-in)

    kent --> kent, *keent 'urine'

The vowel in pik is lengthened to piik, but keep and kent do not lengthen their vowels. The underlying length distinction is clear in the suffixed forms pik-en and keep-in (/-n/ = construct suffix 'of'). Since all three forms are heavy syllables even before lengthening, their

---

[4]It is furthermore shown in McCarthy (1983) that the choice of reduplicative affix is dependent on the mora count of the base not including the final consonant.

different behavior is somewhat mysterious. McCarthy (1983) suggests that if final consonants are extraprosodic, the difference between pi(k) on the one hand and kee(p) and ken(t) on the other becomes apparent: In the latter case, even if the final consonant is not part of the syllable, the syllable is still heavy. Monosyllabic Lengthening can then be understood as making light syllables heavy.

In (15), I give the syllable template of Ponapean and the lexical constraint on codas which disallows all consonantal elements syllable-finally.

(15)

    a. Ponapean syllable template: $_\sigma[\ C\ V\ V\ C\ ]$

    b. Coda Condition:
$$*\ \ \begin{array}{c} C]_\sigma \\ | \\ [+cons] \end{array}$$

Assuming doubly linked structures for geminates (11) and homorganic NC clusters (12), coda syllabification is not hindered by condition (15b) in these cases. The representations in (16) show the syllabification at the word level.

(16) Word-Level Syllabification

a.
```
      σ       σ
     /|\     /|
    C V C   C V
    | |  \ /  |
    n a    p  a
```
nappa
'Chinese cabbage'

b.
```
      σ         σ    Ex
     /|\       /|     |
    C V N     C V    C
    | |  \ /   |     |
    l i   pʷ   o     t
```
limʷpʷot
'five oblong things'

c.
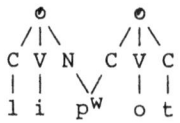

emp
'coconut crab'

Language-specific Extraprosodicity licenses the final consonants at the word level, and postlexically the final segments can be adjoined because Structure Preservation no longer holds and the syllable conditions in (15) can be violated.

(17) Postlexical Syllabification:

a. (identical with (16a))

b.
```
      σ         σ
     /|\       /|\
    C V N     C V C
    | |  \ /  | | |
    l i   pʷ  o   t
```
limʷpʷot
'five oblong things'

(17cont.)
   c.

```
    σ
   /\\
  V N C
  | |/
  e p
```
                              emp
                              'coconut crab'

Notice that the analysis of Ponapean syllable structure has so far been identical to that proposed for Diola in chapter 3, section 3.1. Important differences due to the operation of epenthesis in Ponapean arise when unsyllabifiable segments are encountered during the lexical derivation.

In a syllable-mapping approach to epenthesis, stray epenthesis can be formulated as in (18).

(18)   Map stray consonant to syllable template.

The application of (18) is illustrated by the derivation of /kitik-men/ (19) (with the stem /kitik/ 'rat' and the enclitic /-men/ 'a (of animate beings).' Each step of the derivation is explained below.

(19)
   <u>Lexical</u>:

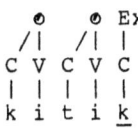
```
         σ   σ  Ex
        /|  /| |
        C V C V C
        | | | | |
        k i t i k
```

(19cont.)
  Word level:

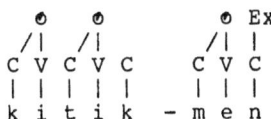

Stray
Epenthesis
(18)

Stray
Erasure   inapplicable

  Postlexical:

Syll
and
Default
```
     σ    σ    σ    σ
    /|   /|   /|   /|\
    C V  C V  C V  C V C
    | |  | |  | |  | | |
    k i  t i  k i  m e n
```

- When the enclitic -men is added at the word level, the stem-final k, no longer being the rightmost element, loses its exprosodic status.

- Structure Preservation prohibits the segment k from being syllabified as a coda of the preceding syllable because of the Coda Condition (15b) and as part of the onset of the following syllable because of the syllable template (15a).

-Epenthesis (18) supplies a syllable to the previously stray segment. Notice that this is the minimal syllable consistent with the syllabification conditions of Ponapean. In particular, k cannot be syllabified as a coda, since this would again violate Structure Preservation.

-Stray Erasure is no longer applicable since all segments are prosodically licensed.

-In the postlexical phonology, the final consonant is syllabified (see (17)) and the default vowel is supplied.

Let us compare this analysis with an analysis under the skeletal rule approach. The skeletal rule needed for Ponapean epenthesis is given in (20).

(20)

$$\emptyset \longrightarrow V \;/\; C' \underline{}$$

The relevant portion of the derivation of kitikimen is given in (21).

(21)
  a. Syllabification:

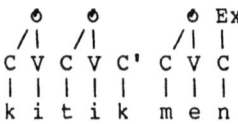

  b. Rule (20):

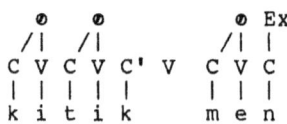

(21cont.)

c. Syllabification:

```
 σ   σ   σ   σ  Ex
/|  /|  /|  /| |
C V C V C V C V C
| | | | | | | | |
k i t i k(i)m e n
```

The medial consonant is left stray after syllabification, and rule (20) inserts a V-slot (21b). Later syllabification builds the medial syllable (21c). This account, although consistent with the facts, is problematic in that it contains certain redundancies. Notice that the environment of the skeletal rule in (20) clearly duplicates the syllable structure conditions of Ponapean, which requires medial (singly-linked) consonants to be onsets (and not codas). The skeletal epenthesis rule in (20) must stipulate that a V-slot is supplied to the <u>right</u> of C', where it can eventually become an onset. The rule basically pre-establishes syllabifiability before syllabification and thus encodes once again the restrictions of Ponapean syllable structure.

Since skeletal rules are not intrinsically related to syllable structure, we can imagine a language with the same syllabification conditions as Ponapean but having a different skeletal rule such as that given in (22), where a V-slot is inserted to the <u>left</u> of the stray consonant.

(22)   ∅ ---> V / __C'

Consider the derivation with this skeletal rule.

(23)
  a. Syllabification:
```
            σ        σ
           /|       /|
          C V  C'  C V
```

  b. Rule (22):
```
            σ         σ
           /|        /|
          C V  V  C' C V
```

  c. Syllabification:
```
         σ  σ      σ                   σ         σ
        /| |      /|         or       /|\       /|
        C V V  C' C V                C V V  C'  C V
```

The stray segment cannot be syllabified even after the rule (22) has applied. It seems that such a skeletal rule would never be posited in a language with the syllabification conditions of Ponapean. However, this gap is unexplained within the skeletal rule approach itself, and it appears necessary to appeal to some functional notion like that of phonological <u>conspiracy</u> (see Kisseberth 1970 and related work). The arguments against the linear approach of SPE therefore carry over to a limited extent to the skeletal rule approach insofar as it crucially uses operations defined on linear sequences of skeletal slots. We will return to this point later in this chapter (sections 4.3 and 4.4).

This argument against the skeletal rule approach to epenthesis is similar to the one found in many analyses motivating Stray Erasure, where it is typically argued that statements of syllable conditions are duplicated in the structural environment of consonant deletion rules (e.g. in Cairns & Feinstein 1982, Steriade 1982, Harris 1983, etc.).

No duplication of this kind is found in the syllable-mapping approach to epenthesis because we can directly appeal to the independently necessary syllable conditions, which already determine where the nuclear position of the vowel will be with respect to the stray consonant.

4.1.2 Melody Spread and Stray Epenthesis

In this section, I will consider the position of syllable-mapping epenthesis in the derivation and its interaction with other phonological rules. The crucial cases are those where epenthesis is bled by the creation of doubly-linked structures making coda syllabification posssible.

The relevant rule in Ponapean is Nasal Assimilation. A coronal nasal assimilates in point of articulation to a following oral or nasal stop as shown in (24).

(24) Coronal Nasal Assimilation

/nan-par/	-->	nampar	'trade wind season'
/tiin-kidi/	-->	tiiŋkidi	'bone of a dog'
/nan-pʷuɲara/	-->	namʷpʷuɲara	'between them'
/kilin-malek/	-->	kilimmalek	'skin of a chicken'
/paan-ɲeteɲete/	->	paaɲɲeteɲete	'roof of the mouth'

Nasal Assimilation is formulated as Melody Spread in (25).

(25) Melody Spread

$$\begin{array}{c} [+\text{nasal}] \\ | \\ C. \quad C \\ \neq \;\; \cdot \;\; | \\ | \;\; \cdot | \\ [+\text{cor}] \; [\alpha F] \end{array}$$

If [+coronal] is the default value for nasals and is only later specified, we can omit the [+coronal] specification for the assimilating nasal and define Melody Spread as a feature-filling rule.

The derivation below shows the ordering relationship of Melody Spread and Stray Epenthesis.

(26) a.   b.

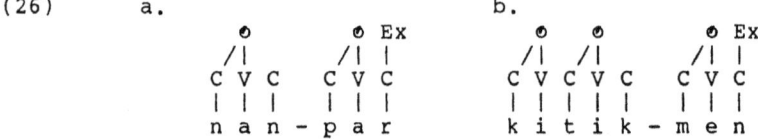

(26cont.)

```
                       σ       σ  Ex
Melody                /|      /| |
Spread:               C V C.  C V C        inapplicable
                      | | ǂ ·.| | |
                      n a n - p a r


                       σ.      σ  Ex
SYLL:                 /| ·.   /| |
                      C V  N C V C          inapplicable
                      | |  \| | |
                      n a   p a r


                                            σ    σ    σ    σ  Ex
Stray                                      /|   /|   /|   /| |
Epenthesis:    inapplicable                C V  C V  C V  C V C
                                           | |  | |  | |  | | |
                                           k i  t i  k    m e n
```

        <u>nampar</u>   <u>kitikimen</u>
   'trade wind season'   'rat'

The application of epenthesis must wait until Melody Spread has created the doubly-linked structure to which coda syllabification immediately applies. If the opposite ordering were posited, with Epenthesis preceding Melody Spread, the latter would never have a chance to apply. The correct ordering is predicted by our hypothesis (see section 4.0) that Stray Epenthesis, like Stray Erasure, is an end-of-cycle operation triggered by the Prosodic Licensing Condition to eliminate unsyllabified material in the string. In our conception, then, epenthesis is formally association of a segment to a syllable template, like ordinary syllable-mapping. However, it differs from the latter in two respects: It is language-particular, and its application is restricted to the end of the cycle and hence not continuous.

4.1.3 OCP Fusion

Besides Melody Spread, there are two other situations in which doubly-linked structures arise.

First, underlying geminates such as <u>kiassi</u> must have a single melody <u>s</u> doubly-linked to the skeleton, as in (27a), and not two <u>s</u> melodies each separately linked to the skeleton, as in (27b).

(27)

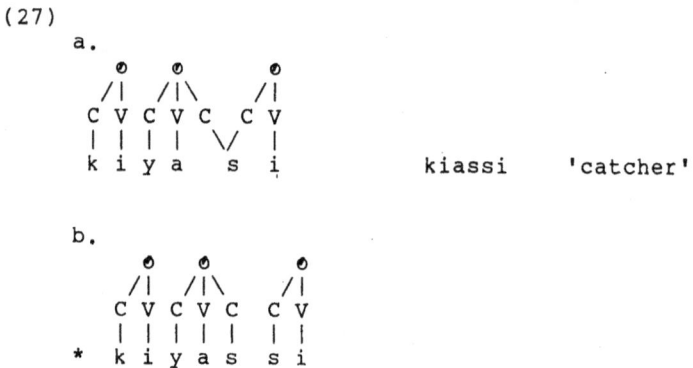

The Obligatory Contour Principle (Leben 1973, Goldsmith 1976), interpreted along lines pursued in McCarthy (1986), predicts that only the monomelodic doubly-linked structure in (27a) will ever occur morpheme-internally.

(28) <u>Obligatory Contour Principle</u> (McCarthy 1979b,81,86)
   At the melodic level, adjacent identical elements are prohibited.

The structure in (27b) as the syllable representation for <u>kiassi</u> is ruled out both by the OCP and by the Ponapean Coda Condition (15b).

The following examples illustrate heteromorphemic geminates.

(29)
   /weid-da/ ---> weidida   'proceed upward'
   /lus-saŋ/ ---> lusisaŋ   'jump from'

While morpheme-internal geminate <u>s</u>, for example, must be monomelodic and doubly linked in the lexicon, two <u>s</u>'s which come together through morpheme concatenation, as in (29), are each singly linked to an independent skeletal slot. This representational contrast is illustrated in (30).

(30) a.   b.

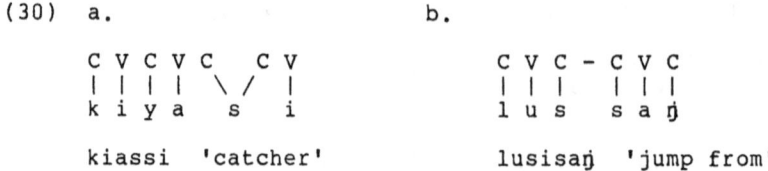

kiassi 'catcher'   lusisaŋ 'jump from'

The heteromorphemic geminate in (30b) has a bimelodic structures, and the Coda Condition is enforced, leading correctly to Stray Epenthesis:

(31)
                    Epenthesis

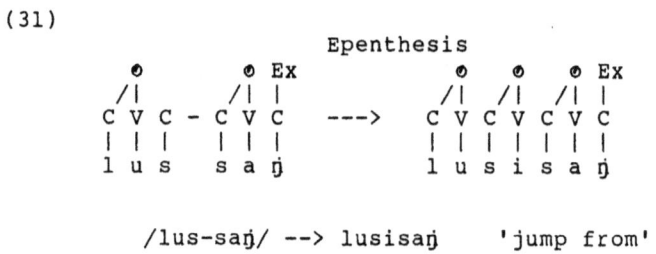

/lus-saŋ/ --> lusisaŋ   'jump from'

The representational difference between derived and underived geminates entailed by the OCP thus seems to account correctly for the facts.

However, it turns out that this behavior of geminates under suffixation is restricted to coronals and constitutes a special case for derived geminates in Ponapean. As shown in (32), when noncoronal homorganic consonants, either oral or nasal, become adjacent through morpheme concatenation, there is no epenthesis. Instead a process of Nasal Substitution takes place, and the first consonant becomes a nasal sharing position of articulation and velarization with the second consonant (Rehg and Sohl 1981:61). Notice that Nasal Substitution occurs in suffixation (32) and in reduplication (33). Furthermore, reduplication differs from suffixation in that in reduplicated forms even the coronals are not split by epenthesis but undergo Nasal Substitution (33c-g).

(32)

a. /kehp-m^wot/ --> kehm^wm^wot 'variety of yam'
b. /ep-p^woatol/ --> em^wp^woatol 'game'
c. /sap^w-paa/ --> sampaa 'world, earth'
d. /ak-keelail/ --> aŋkeelail 'demonstrate strength'

(33)

a. /pap-pap/ --> pampap 'swimming'
b. /kik-kik/ --> kiŋkik 'kicking'
c. /tat-tat/ --> tantat 'writhe'
d. /sas-sas/ --> sansas 'stagger'
e. /dil-dil/ --> dindil 'penetrate'
f. /sel-sel/ --> sensel 'tied'
g. /sar-sar/ --> sansar 'fade'

Interpreting the term 'nasal substitution' literally would lead us to expect a process which merely inserts a nasal feature in the first of two adjacent homorganic consonants. This interpretation is informally given below.

(34)

Notice that this does not explain why there is no epenthesis in the cases where Nasal Substitution has taken place. Since the nasal consonant is still singly linked to the skeleton, coda syllabification should be disallowed, and we expect epenthesis to apply.

What we need is a <u>fusion</u> mechanism, operating after or simultaneous with morpheme concatenation, which creates the doubly-linked structure (35b) from the singly-linked structure (35a) and enables coda syllabification to take place.

(35)   a.   Fusion   b.

```
          C   C                    C   C
          |   |      --->           \ /
          p   p                      p
```

In this approach, Nasal Substitution is an operation inserting a nasal feature when a doubly-linked structure arises.

(36)   Nasal Substitution:

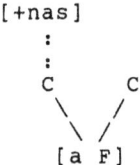

The fact that Nasal Substitution (36) does not apply to the morpheme-internal geminates (see (37)) is expected under the Strict Cycle, which blocks the application of the rule in underived environments.

(37)

kiassi	'catcher'	*	kiansi
nappa	'Chinese cabbage'	*	nampa
kakko	'putting on airs'	*	kaŋko

Under the assumptions of McCarthy (1986), the OCP itself is not an active 'glomming' mechanism. Assuming that all morphemes initially occupy separate morphological tiers, it has been proposed (Younes 1983, McCarthy 1986) that a process of Tier Conflation is needed to linearize the melody elements. McCarthy (1986) further suggests that Conflation may also fuse two identical consonants into a single melodic unit, as shown in the hypothetical example /dab-ba/ (38).

(38)
```
                b a     Tier
                | |   Conflation
        C V C + C V     -->      C V C   C V
        | | |                    | |  \ /  |
        d a b                    d a   b   a
```

I suggest that the effects evidenced in (32) and (33) are results of Tier Conflation with Fusion. Our analysis of Ponapean syllable structure, which requires codas to be doubly linked, thus provides phonological evidence, although of a theory-internal nature, in favor of this interpretation of Tier Conflation.

A final point which must be settled concerns secondary articulation for labials, namely velarization. When two labials with different values for velarization come together, the first labial is not only subject to Nasal Substitution but also receives the velarization value of the second labial. Thus in (39a) the underlying sequences p^w+p becomes $m+p$, and in (39b) $p+p^w$ becomes m^w+p^w.

(39)
    a.   /sap^w-paa/ --> sampaa   'world, earth'

    b.   /ep-p^{w}oatol/ --> em^{w}p^{w}oatol   'game'

This can be understood if further tier structure is recognized and secondary articulation does not count for determining identity when Fusion/Tier Conflation takes place (see Mester 1986 for such an approach). We can assume that primary place of articulation occupies an independent tier to which velarization is linked as a secondary articulation. This is informally indicated in (41a). When two labials adjacent across a morpheme boundary differ in velarization, Fusion/Conflation on the primary place tier results in two velarization features linked to a single melodic slot (41b). The Velar Delinking rule in (40) delinks the first of the doubly-linked units (41c).

(40) Velar Delinking:

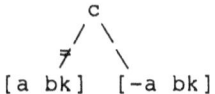
[a bk] [-a bk]

For the sake of clarity, the derivation below does not indicate syllabification. As soon as the double linking arises by Tier Conflation, coda syllabification can take place, so epenthesis has no chance to apply.

(41)
a.

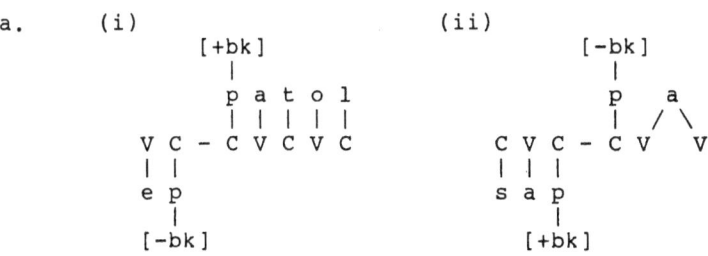

(41cont.)
b. Tier
   Conflation:

```
       V C   C V C V C              C V C   C V   V
       | \ / | | | |                | | \ / \ /
       e  p   a t o l               s a  p    a
         / \                           / \
       [-bk] [+bk]                   [+bk] [-bk]
```

c. Velar
   Delinking:

```
       V N   C V C V C              C V N   C V   V
       | \ / | | | |                | | \ / \ /
       e  p   a t o l               s a  p    a
         ≠ \                           ≠ \
       [-bk] [+bk]                   [+bk] [-bk]
```

d. Nasal
   Subst:

```
          [+nas]                       [+nas]
            :                            :
       V C   C V C V C              C V C   C V   V
       | \ / | | | |                | | \ / \ /
       e  p   a t o l               s a  p    a
           \                             \
       [-bk] [+bk]                   [+bk] [-bk]
```

e. Stray
   Epen: inapplicable   inapplicable

f. Stray
   Erasure:

```
       V N   C V C V C              C V N   C V   V
       | \ / | | | |                | | \ / \ /
       e  p   a t o l               s a  p    a
           \                             \
       ∅  [+bk]                      ∅  [-bk]

       emʷpʷotol                     sampaa
```

What remains to be accounted for is the apparently schizophrenic behavior of coronal geminates. Recall that

coronal geminates derived by suffixation undergo Epenthesis
(42), whereas those derived by reduplication undergo Nasal
Substitution (43).

(42)

/weid-da/   --> weidida   'proceed upward'

/lus-saŋ/   --> lusisaŋ   'jump from'

(43)

/tat-tat/   --> tantat   'writhe'

/sas-sas/   --> sansas   'stagger'

The fusion analysis given above does not directly
account for this difference in coronal behavior. We can
attempt an explanation with some additional assumptions:
The level of suffixation precedes the level of
reduplication and coronals are not specified for coronality
during the level of suffixation. The identity requirement
needed for Fusion is then not met because of
Underspecification.[5] At the level of reduplication the
default specification of coronals has taken place and their

---

[5]This assumes that identity is only established by real
feature specifications, such that two unspecified segments
do not count as identical. The unspecified nature of
coronals is supported by Nasal Assimilation, where only
the coronal nasals assimilate. If coronals are
unspecified, Nasal Assimilation can be considered a
feature-filling operation, as discussed above.

identity can now be determined by Fusion/Tier Conflation. Like the noncoronals they fuse into doubly-linked structures undergoing Nasal Substitution and allow coda syllabification to take place.

4.2 Epenthesis in Sino-Japanese Morphemes

In dealing with Japanese syllable structure in chapter 2, our concern was to give an analysis which correctly generates the possible syllables of Japanese. Japanese syllables can only be closed by nasals and by consonants which are part of a geminate (e.g. [nip][pon] 'Japan'). The syllable analysis given in chapter 2 is repeated in (44).

(44) Japanese syllable template: [C V V C]

  Coda Condition:[6]   * $C]_\sigma$
                                |
                            [-nasal]

---

[6] It should be noted that word-medial coda nasals are also always homorganic to the following consonant, and word-final nasals take on a vocalic character. It may therefore be possible to generalize the Japanese Coda Condition even further to exclude all consonantal units syllable-finally as in Ponapean or Diola.

I will argue that the interesting phonological behavior of Sino-Japanese compounds[7] characterized in McCawley (1968) is to be understood as involving epenthesis (and not syncope), and that the gemination effects occurring at Sino-Japanese morpheme boundaries result from Tier Conflation as well as from a rule of spreading. The account is very similar to the one given for Ponapean (section 4.1), and I will be contrasting the two analyses at relevant points. One difference lies in the fact that no word-level extraprosodicity effects are found in Japanese.

---

[7]Sino-Japanese compounding is a productive word-formation process in Modern Japanese. Compared to the ideophonic (onomatopoetic) and the foreign vocabulary (e.g. from English, and other European languages), the Sino-Japanese phonology is closest to the Yamato (native) phonology (see McCawley 1968 and Itô & Mester 1986 for discussion).

4.2.1 Syncope versus epenthesis

The syncope rule proposed by McCawley (1968) to account for final V/Ø alternations in Sino-Japanese morphemes is informally given in (45) (the Sino-Japanese morpheme boundary is indicated by the [+]-notation).

(45) Sino-Japanese Vowel Syncope:

$$V \longrightarrow \emptyset \; / \; k \; \underline{} \; + \; k$$

The final vowels of <u>gaku</u> '(relating to) scholarship' and <u>seki</u> '(relating to) stone' elide when the following morpheme starts with <u>k</u> as shown in (46a) and (47a). The examples in (46b) and (47b) illustrate that elision does not occur in any other situation.

(46)
   a.   gak+koo   'school'   (cf. *gak$\underline{u}$+koo)

       gak+kai   'academic conference' (cf. *gak$\underline{u}$+kai)

   b.   gak$\underline{u}$+see   'student'

       gak$\underline{u}$+čoo   'school president'

       gak$\underline{u}$+batsu   'academic clique'

       gak$\underline{u}$+mon   'learning'

       dai+gak$\underline{u}$ 'university'

       gak$\underline{u}$+in   'school, academy'

(47)

a. sek+ken,   'soap'   (cf. *seki+ken)

   sek+ki,   'stoneware'   (cf. *seki+ki)

b. seki+tan   'coal'

   seki+yu   'petroleum'

   tan+seki   'gallstone'

   seki+en   'rock salt'

The syncope rule (45) applies to kVk, yielding the geminate kk. This is a very unusual type of syncope in light of the antigemination effect of the OCP discussed in McCarthy (1986): Syncope rules are regularly blocked in contexts where their application would result in violations of the OCP. The rule in (45) in fact appears to obey exactly the opposite constraint, it applies only to vowels flanked by identical consonants.

I will argue for a syllable-based analysis in which the alternations in (46) and (47) are treated as results not of syncope but of epenthesis. The hypothesis is that the underlying forms of these morphemes do not contain a final vowel. Thus the forms in (46b) and (47b) are considered to be derived forms having undergone epenthesis.[8]

Before dealing with the problems facing an epenthesis approach, I will briefly sketch the main point of the analysis by contrasting the derivations of the forms gakusee and gakkoo.

The underlying forms involved are gak, see, and koo. As in Ponapean, I assume that Fusion via Tier Conflation takes place in gakkoo, resulting in a doubly-linked structure with a single k, which can in turn be fully syllabified according to the conditions in (44).

```
(48)          k o       Fusion              SYLL      σ       σ
              | |\                                    /|\     /|\
       C V C - C V V  --->  C V C   C V V  --->  C V C   C V V
       | | |                | |  \ /  |/         | |  \/   |/
       g a k                g a   k   o          g a  k    o
```

For gak+see, Tier Conflation does not result in any doubly linked structure. The morpheme-final k cannot be syllabified because of the Coda Condition and the stray k is mapped to a new syllable, as indicated in (49).

---

[8]Tateishi (1986) has independently proposed a similar analysis in a detailed study of Sino-Japanese compounds. He furthermore shows that the morphemes in question behave accentually like monosyllables with respect to the preaccenting rule of Japanese. Tateishi's (1986) analysis confirms our hypothesis that these cases should be analyzed as involving insertion of an epenthetic vowel and not deletion of an underlying vowel.

(49)
```
      σ         σ              σ    σ    σ
     /|        /|\            /|   /|   /|\
   C V C  -  C V V    --->   C V C V   C V V
   | | |     | |/            | | |     | |/
   g a k     s e             g a k     s e
```

4.2.2 Quality of epenthetic vowels and epenthesis contexts

In pursuing an epenthesis account instead of a syncope account, two factors must be dealt with. First, the epenthetic vowel can be either [i] or [u] as shown in (46b) and (47b). Second, epenthesis takes place not only to break up medial consonant clusters but also finally (e.g. dai+gak<u>u</u>) and when the second morpheme is vowel-initial (e.g. gak<u>u</u>+in).

The answer to the first problem lies in the suggestion made by Martin (1952) and discussed by McCawley (1968) that palatalization is dinstinctive in Japanese consonants (except before [i], where consonants are always palatalized). Consider the following minimal pairs:

(50)

k^{y}aku	'guest'	kaku	'nucleus'
k^{y}oku	'tune'	koku	'country'
k^{y}uu	'urgent'	kuu	'space'
k^{y}i[9]	'tree'		

Similar pairs exist for the other consonants: s̲, š̲, n̲, n̲^{y}, m̲, m̲^{y}, etc.

Since lexical distinctions must in any case be made on the consonants to account for these minimal pairs, it is natural to assume that a lexical distinction can also be encoded on morpheme-final consonants, marking them either as palatalized, as in /sek^y/, or as nonpalatalized, as in /gak/. The inserted vowel will be i̲ after a palatalized morpheme-final consonant and u̲ after a nonpalatalized consonant. The explanation here is parallel to the one given for Ponapean epenthesis, where the velarization of the following consonant determines the quality of the epenthetic vowel.

I assume that palatalization, as a secondary articulation, occupies a separate tier and therefore does not count in determining 'identity' for the purposes of Fusion/Tier Conflation. To account for the fact that the

---

[9]This is usually simplified to k̲i̲ because palatalization is nondistincitive before i̲.

palatalization of the geminates resulting from fusion is determined by the second consonant, a delinking rule similar to the one proposed for Ponapean can be invoked. In (51) and (52), I show how the second consonant is responsible for the value of palatalization for the geminate created by fusion.

(51) gak-k^{y}uu --> gak^{y}k^{y}uu   'class'

```
        [+high]
           |
          k u
          | |\
C V C - C V V      --->    C V C   C V V
| | |     |                | |  \ / |/
g a k                      g a   k  u
    |                          ≠ \
 [-high]                   [-hi] [+hi]
```

(52) sek^y-koo --> sekkoo

```
        [-high]
           |
          k o
          | |\
C V C - C V V      --->    C V C   C V V
| | |     |                | |  \ / |/
s e k                      s e   k  o
    |                          ≠ \
 [+high]                   [+hi] [-hi]
```

What remains to be accounted for is the fact that epenthetic vowels appear not only medially to break up consonant clusters, but in two additional contexts:

(i) word-finally after consonants, and (ii) medially after consonants before vowel-initial morphemes.

The occurrence of word-final epenthesis is a consequence of the fact that there is no word-level Extraprosodicity in Japanese. Since all segments must be syllabically licensed at the word level, another syllable is assigned to final stray consonants as in (53).

(53)
```
     σ       σ              σ      σ    σ
    /|\     /|              /|\    /|   /|
   C V V   C V C    --->   C V V  C V  C V
   | | |   | | |           | | |  | |  | :
   d a i   g a k           d a i  g a  k u
```

To account for the occurrence of epenthesis in cases where the second morpheme begins with a vowel, we need one additional assumption on syllabification. Notice that the morpheme-final <u>k</u> is not syllabified as an onset in (54).

(54)
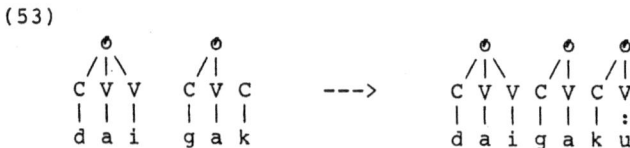

One possibility would be to posit an initial glottal stop (<u>gak-ʔin</u>) blocking onset syllabification for the preceding consonant. Such a glottal stop, however, appears to be unwarranted from phonetic evidence (see Poser 1984 for discussion). I will therefore assume that syllabification simply cannot cross Sino-Japanese morpheme boundaries.

Consider finally the t-final morphemes in (55), where all sequences of voiceless consonants become geminates.

(55)

/bet-taku/	->	bettaku	'detached villa'
/bet-kaku/	->	bekkaku	'different style'
/bet-puu/	->	beppuu	'separate cover'
/bet-šitu/	->	beššitu	'separate room'

Recall that in Ponapean we found a similar kind of overlap between Nasal Substitution and Nasal Assimilation: The former applied in the configuration C_1C_2, where $C_1 = C_2$, and the latter in the configuration nC. The situation in Japanese seems parallel, with identical consonants in the one case and tC in the other. We can assume that morpheme-final [t] is unspecified and that the unmarked values for all features are supplied at a later point. At the time of morpheme concatenation the following consonants can spread into the unspecified C-slot by a rule of Melody Spread.

The two possible ways of achieving a multiply linked

structure, by Fusion and by Spreading are then attested in both Japanese and Ponapean.[10]

4.2.3 Parameters and typology

In terms of syllabification, Japanese fills the last gap in the paradigm for the parameters of word level Eextraprosodicity and Stray Epenthesis which are set on a language-specific basis. As (56) shows, the two parameters are clearly independent.

(56)

	Diola	Ponapean	Lardil	Japanese
Word-Level Extraprosodicity	on	on	off	off
Stray Epenthesis	off	on	off	on

Stray Erasure is not a parameter but is considered to be universally 'on'.[11]

---

[10] See Mester (1986) for the contention that both fusion and spreading are independently necessary mechanisms in multitiered phonology.

[11] In chapter 5, we will discuss the Icelandic system, where the two stray operations crucially interact.

4.3 Skeletal Rules and Syllable Structure

The argument against positing skeletal rules for the Ponapean epenthesis phenomenon in 4.1 was that the environment specification of the skeletal rule duplicates independently necessary syllable structure conditions. A possible counterargument to this would be found if certain skeletal rules are indeed independent of syllable structure, such that a significant generalization is gained by positing a skeletal rule. Levin (1985) presents an interesting case in this regard. The evidence comes from Axininca Campa, an Arawakan language spoken in the Amazon jungle (Payne 1981). In the nonlinear framework, various aspects of Axininca phonology have been discussed in Yip (1983), Levin (1985), and McCarthy and Prince (1985). In Axininca, the vowel a is inserted inside consonant clusters (CC -> CaC) and the consonant t is inserted between two vowels (VV -> VtV). Payne (1981) notes that a and t are the unmarked segments of the language and that epenthesis is a very general process breaking vowel hiatus and resolving consonant clustering.[12] Illustrative examples

---

[12]Payne (1981) collapses the two rules by means of the feature [syllabic] and the alpha-notation:

$\emptyset$ --> [a syll] / [-a syll] _____ [-a syll]

appear in (57) ([c] = apical affricate ([ȼ] in Payne 1981)).

(57) a-epenthesis

			'I will really ___'
	/noN-kim-piro-i/	-> noŋkim<u>a</u>piro<u>t</u>i	'... hear'
	/noN-c^hitok-piro-i/	-> nonc^hitok<u>a</u>piro<u>t</u>i	'... hit'
	/noN-pok-piro-i/	-> nompok<u>a</u>piro<u>t</u>i	'... come'
cf.	/noN-pisi-piro-i/	-> nompisipiro<u>t</u>i	'... sweep'
	/noN-piyo-piro-i/	-> nompiyopiro<u>t</u>i	'... heap'

(58) t-epenthesis:

	/noN-pisi-i/	--> nompisi<u>t</u>i	'I will sweep'
	/noN-piyo-i/	--> nompiyo<u>t</u>i	'I will heap'
cf.	/noN-kim-i/	--> noŋkimi	'I will hear'
	/noN-c^hitok-i/	--> nonc^hitoki	'I will hit'
	/noN-pok-i/	--> nompoki	'I will come'

After considering how a syllable-based analysis of Axininca proceeds, I will return to the interesting proposal on conditions on skeletal rules in Levin (1985).

Payne (1981) describes the Axininca syllable structure as $CVVN$, where N is the nasal archisegment which always assimilates to the following consonant. We can posit the Coda Condition as in (59).

(59)   Axininca Campa Syllable Analysis

Syllable structure: [C V V C]

Coda condition: *   C]$_\sigma$
                      |
                   [+cons]

Onset: obligatory

Different from the cases that we have seen so far, the onset consonant is lexically required in Axininca.[13] Structure Preservation ensures that onsetless syllables do not arise during the lexical derivation. The syllable template which is mapped to the segments contains not only the universally obligatory nuclear slot but also the language specific obligatory onset position, in our terms at least [CV]. The derivation of nompokapiroti 'I will really come' is given below.

---

[13]Axininca permits onsetless syllables in word-initial position. Some version of initial extraprosodicity might be invoked to account for this. We could assume that the domain in which all syllables must satisfy the syllable structure conditions starts from the head (i.e. the vowel) of the initial syllable. This requires word-medial syllables to have onsets.

(60)

Syllabification

Default Insertion

nompok<u>a</u>piro<u>t</u>i   'I will really come'

   This analysis of Axininca epenthesis relies solely
on the independently needed syllable structure conditions.
The obligatoriness of the onset, that is, the fact that
the absolutely minimal expansion of a syllable node in
Axininca is [CV], directly entails both vowel and consonant
epenthesis in the appropriate contexts under the
syllable-mapping theory of epenthesis.

   Levin (1985) argues that Axininca provides a strong
argument for a purely skeletal rule using the X-notation.
In the skeletal rule approach to epenthesis reference to
syllable structure makes it impossible to collapse
V-epenthesis and C-epenthesis into a single rule but a
X-skeletal rule can be simply stated as in (61)
(morphological information is suppressed for clarity).

(61) Epenthesis in Axininca Campa

$\emptyset \longrightarrow X \:/\: X \underline{} X$

This rule, when combined with the following conditions on the structural description and structural change of skeletal rules, yields the desired interpretation.

(62)

Conditions on X-tier transformations (Levin 1985:331)
All rules RX are of the form:
Delete/ Insert X / Y__Z, where
  i. X, Y, Z must be single skeletal slots;
 ii. $\{X\} \:\hat{}\: \{X', \underline{X}\} \neq \emptyset$;
iii. $\{Y,Z\} \:\hat{}\: \{X', \underline{X}\} \neq \emptyset$;
 iv. the output of of RX is subject to the following filters:
    a. * $\underline{X}\:\underline{X}$ b. * X' X'
and where the representation of other tiers is optional.

The Axininca skeletal rule (61) inserts an X-slot between two X-slots. Crucial for the interpretation of rule (61) is the output filter in (62iv), which ensures that the rule does <u>not</u> result in a consonant being inserted next to another consonant (i.e. *X'X'= * C C), nor a vowel being inserted next to a vowel (i.e. *$\underline{X}\:\underline{X}$ = * V V).

The condition (62) rules out skeletal rules such as those given in (63), which never seem to be attested.

(63)
    a. ∅ --> C / C'___   (Insert a consonant after a stray consonant)

    b. V --> ∅ / ___ C'   (Delete a vowel before a stray consonant)

    c. ∅ --> C / V___   (Insert a consonant after a vowel)

While the rule in (61) does not carry information which duplicate the Axininca syllable structure, it appears that the condition (62iv) exactly prohibits highly marked syllables from arising. The output filter (*VV, and *CC) ensures that skeletal rules always improve the syllabic wellformedness of the string. Since syllable structure conditions (both universal and language specific) are independently needed in the grammar, this condition, while expressing a valid generalization, lacks explanatory force.[14]

---

[14]There is one other relevant point. Payne (1981, 145) notes that "any time a CV verb is preceded by word-boundary and followed by a consonant-initial suffix, there is addition of a syllable /ta/ consisting of the unmarked consonant and unmarked vowel, appearing somewhat like a 'double epenthesis'." Consider the root na 'carry' in the following forms.

(i)
a.
/no-na-wai-i/ --> nonawaiti   'I will continue to carry'

/no-na-piro-i/ --> nonapiroti   'I will carry it well.'

b.
/na-wai-aaNc^{h}i/ --> natawaitaanc^{h}i   'to carry continually'

/na-piro-aaNc^{h}i/ --> natapirotaanc^{h}i   'to carry well'

The examples in (i b), in which the root occurs without prefixes, illustrate the double epenthesis phenomenon. In (i a) the root does not undergo double epenthesis because of the presence of the prefix no-. Under the assumption that the insertion of ta is accomplished by two applications of the epenthesis rule, it is interesting that the Axininca skeletal rule (61) guided by the conditions (62) will fail to apply since the first application of insertion will always violate the output filter.

4.4 Concluding Remarks

In this chapter, I have shown that skeletal operations independent of syllable structure lead to redundancy in various respects. Since skeletal rules are assumed to be normal phonological rules, the null assumption must be that they have all the properties of phonological rules. Some condition then becomes necessary to capture their unexpectedly limited distribution. While the conditions on X-tier transformations (62) express valid generalizations, they merely give a list of possible types of rules and are not truly explanatory.

In a syllable-mapping analysis, there is no necessity for such complex conditions. The epenthesis sites are determined by the language-specific syllable conditions, guided by Structure Preservation and Prosodic Licensing. Given that a syllable-mapping analysis of epenthesis is only compatible with a template-approach, this constitutes another argument for a syllable theory in which language-specific conditions on syllabification are stated in the grammar in terms of conditions on representation.

CHAPTER V
DIRECTIONALITY IN SYLLABIFICATION

5.0 Introduction

In mapping syllables to phonological strings, a certain amount of indeterminacy arises in the syllabic parsing of intervocalic consonants. One of the claimed advantages of a rule-approach to syllabification (Steriade 1982) is the ordering possibility of the Onset rule and the Coda rule: Ordering the Onset Rule before the Coda Rule maximizes the onset, the opposite ordering maximizes the coda.

In this chapter, I will argue that a template-approach coupled with a directionality parameter, adequately accounts for aspects of syllabification which previously needed extrinsically ordered syllable-building rules or nonlocal evaluation metrics.[1]

---

[1] The idea of directional syllabification is not new and has been proposed in different theoretical contexts by Kenstowicz et.al. (1982) for Kabyle Berber, Steriade (1984) for Rumanian, Noske (1985) for Yawelmani, ter Mors (1985) for Klamath, and Dell & Elmedlaoui (1985) for Tashlhiyt Berber.

It is universally true that a single intervocalic consonant is always analyzed as an onset. I will call this the Principle of CV-precedence.

(1)   Principle of CV-Precedence

   A consonant immediately preceding a vowel is universally an onset.

This principle can be encoded in Universal Grammar in a number of ways. In a rule-approach (Steriade 1982) maximally unmarked CV syllables are formed by a universal first rule (2) in the sequence of syllable-building rules.

(2)   Core CV-rule:

$$C\ V \longrightarrow \overset{\overset{\sigma}{/|}}{C\ V}$$

   (Onset/Rime nodes suppressed)

Since the string is initially parsed by this rule, all intervocalic C's will become onsets before rules creating codas become applicable.

It does not follow from the rule-approach itself, however, that the CV-rule is universal or that it is the first rule among the syllabification rules. The generalization about the CV-sequence being the universally unmarked syllable and the rule-approach to syllabification are not intrinsically related, as is sometimes assumed. In the rule-approach, it is still a stipulation that the core syllable rule is universal and that it cannot follow any coda rules.

Therefore, a template-approach with a special provision for CV-syllables is neither more nor less stipulative than the rule-approach with a universal Core CV-rule which is always ordered as the first rule. I propose the following positive universal Core Syllable Condition:

(3) Universal Core Syllable Condition (UCSC)

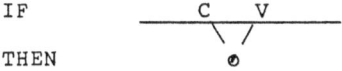

('The sequence CV must belong to a single syllable.')

The Core Syllable Condition (3) works like other syllable conditions such as the coda conditions. It guides initial syllabification so that CV-sequences are always tautosyllabic, and if a structure violating this universal condition arises during the lexical derivation as shown in the hypothetical example (4), dissociation (desyllabification) takes place. Subsequent reassociation (resyllabification) makes the CV-sequence tautosyllabic.

(4)

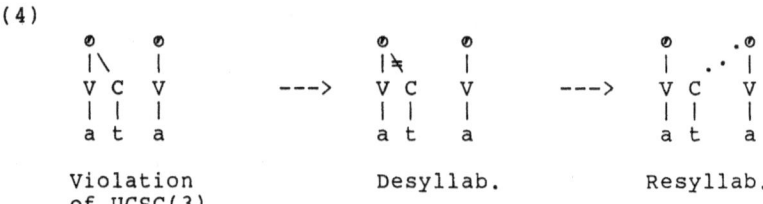

    Violation   Desyllab.   Resyllab.
    of UCSC(3)

The Core Syllable Condition (3) in the template-approach is then equivalent to the Core CV-rule (2) in the rule-approach.

There is still the question of how to disambiguate longer intervocalic consonant clusters. For example, in a language whose syllable template allows both codas and complex onsets (e.g. [CCVC]), a consonantal sequence can be parsed either as a complex onset (e.g. V.CCV) or as coda + simple onset (e.g. VC.CV). Both types of parsings are observed (the former in many Indoeuropean languages where onsets tend to maximize, and the latter in e.g. Klamath). Such differences are accounted for in the rule-approach through stipulated ordering of Onset rule and Coda rule. The ordering: Onset rule, Coda rule yields the complex onset, while the opposite ordering yields coda + simple onset.

Instead of stipulated ordering, we will appeal to the prosodic principle of Directionality. As a parameter of syllabification, syllable mapping proceeding directionally from left to right or from right to left yields exactly the same result as the ordering between Onset rule and Coda rule. Onset maximization (e.g. in Indoeuropean languages) results from right-to-left template matching. For example, in (5) the string is maximally matched to the syllable template from right-to-left, so that the complex onset is formed.

(5)

```
V C C V
| | | |
o s t a
```

On the other hand, if the directionality parameter is set as left-to-right, syllable mapping starts from the leftmost end of the string as in (6). Since the syllable template allows a coda, the segment s is now syllabified as part of the leftmost syllable.

(6)

```
V C C V
| | | |
o s t a
```

But notice that even if the syllable template allows two consonants in the coda, the next consonant t would not be incorporated into the initial syllable because the resulting structure (7) violates the Universal Core Syllable Condition (3).

(7)

        Violation of UCSC

Thus right-to-left syllabification results in maximizing the onset and left to right syllabification results in maximizing the coda, modulo the universal condition regarding CV-sequences (3).

 The hypothesis that syllabification is governed by a directionality parameter is preferable to an approach which has recourse to stipulated ordering statements because it brings the theory of syllabification in line with other areas of Prosodic Phonology (like metrical theory, the theory of reduplication, tonology, root-and-pattern morphology, etc.), in all of which directionality is recognized as a fundamental and independently necessary principle of the theory.

 This chapter is organized as follows. In section 5.1, I will take up the syllable-related phonology of

Icelandic. The complex Icelandic system of deletions and insertions will further exemplify the interactions of many of the principles developed in this thesis and will thus serve as a case study.

In section 5.2, further predictions of directional syllabification will be explored. It will be argued that the directionality parameter can solve some of the puzzles regarding epenthesis sites.

5.1 Syllabification in Icelandic - a case study

The phonology of Icelandic has been extensively explored since the earliest work in generative phonology (Andersen 1969, 1974, Orešnik 1972, 1978, etc.). One of the first syllable analyses (Vennemann 1972) within the generative framework is based on Icelandic, and it is one of the languages to which the framework of Lexical Phonology has been applied in some detail (Kiparsky 1984). It will therefore be interesting as well as instructive to see how the prosodic syllable theory developed in this thesis deals with various complex syllable-related aspects of Icelandic phonology.

5.1.1 Icelandic syllable structure

Vennemann (1972) and Kiparsky (1984) convincingly argue that vowel length in Icelandic is phonologically derived and can be analyzed as lengthening in stressed open syllables. Stress in Icelandic falls regularly on the first syllable.

Examples illustrating length distinctions are given in (8). (Forms are cited in Icelandic orthography except when specifically noted otherwise. The digraph ae denotes the short diphthong [ai], and d stands for orthographic ð.) In stressed syllables, vowels followed by a single consonant are long (indicated by macrons), whereas vowels followed by consonant clusters or geminate consonants are short.

(8)

hī.ti	'heat'	hit.ti	'(he) hit'
ō.kur	'usury'	ok.kur	'us'
sū.pa	'to sip'	sup.tu	'sip!'
hō.fud	'head'	har.dur	'hard'
ā.kur	'field'	els.ka	'love'
fā.ra	'ride'	kal.la	'call'

Vowels in monosyllabic words are lengthened if final (9) or followed by a single consonant (10a) but remain short if followed by two consonants (10b).

(9)

    ā   'river'

    skō   'shoe'

    bū   'homestead'

(10)

a.		b.	
hās	'hoarse'	hest	'horse'
nȳr	'new'	björn	'bear'
skīp	'ship'	skips	'ship's'

With Kiparsky (1984), I assume that final consonants are extrametrical, which accounts for the lengthening in monosyllabic words.[2]

One characteristic of Icelandic syllabification is the difference observed among word-internal obstruent-sonorant sequences. Consider the parsing of

---

[2] This is similar to the analysis proposed by McCarthy (1983) for Monosyllabic Noun Lengthening in Ponapean, see section 4.1.

the three minimally different sequences in (11), where only the sequence kr (11b) is tautosyllabic.[3]

(11)
a. V k l V --> V k . l V   (cf. ek.la 'lack')
b. V k r V --> V . k r V   (cf. ē.kra 'field')
c. V g r V --> V g . r V   (cf. haeg.ri 'right' adj. comp.)

More precisely, intervocalic clusters consisting of a tense obstruent {p,t,k,s} followed by {r,v,j} are tautosyllabic, all other intervocalic clusters are heterosyllabic. Some examples illustrating the difference in syllabification are given in (12).

(12)
a. Tautosyllabic medial clusters:

snū.pra	'chide'
sö.tra	'sweet gen.pl'
vö.kva	'water'
tvī.svar	'twice'
ē.sja	'a mountain'
vē.kja	'awaken'
vī.tja	'visit'

---

[3]This is not the parsing found in related languages (e.g. German, English, and the Scandinavian languages), where all three obstruent-sonorant sequences in (11) are tautosyllabic.

b. Heterosyllabic medial clusters:

    ep.li   'apple'
    es.ki   'ash'
    sig.la   'sail'
    haeg.ri   'right'
    af.laga   'out of order'
    vel.ja   'choose'
    tem.ja   'domesticate'

The assumption made in Kiparsky (1984:153) is that "[the] clusters [in (12a)] constitute permissible onsets and are syllabified with the following vowel [JI]." Although this accounts for the difference in parsing of the intervocalic clusters in (12), we face a problem with the implicit assumption that the clusters in (12b) do not constitute permissible onsets, given the fact that they are clearly allowed as onsets in word-initial position:

(13)
    klifa   'climb'   flaska   'bottle'
    plata   'plate'   fjos   'cattle'
    blað   'leaf'   fru   'Mrs'
    brekka   'slope'   rjuka   'smoke'
    draga   'to draw'   njota   'enjoy'
    dvergur   'dwarf'   mjolk   'milk'
    djöfull   'devil'   ljotur   'ugly'
    skap   'temper'   stafa   'spell'

These word-initial clusters cannot be accounted for by assuming initial extraprosodicity for several reasons. First, notice that - except for sC-clusters - the sonority requirement (rising sonority in onsets) is strictly observed.[4] If the initial consonant is extraprosodic, no sonority requirement of this kind is expected.

Secondly, since extraprosodicity is defined on a single prosodic constituent (i.e. segment, syllable, foot, etc.), it cannot account for the occurrence of triconsonantal initial clusters as in (14).

(14)
    brjost   'breast'
    drjupa   'to drip'
    fljota   'to float'
    smjör   'butter'
    snjor   'snow'

Even with initial extraprosodicity licensing the first consonant in (14), the remaining cluster would not be one of the permitted onset clusters in (12a).

Finally, it seems that the clusters parsed heterosyllabically in (12b) can be tautosyllabic in

---

[4] I am following the standard assumption made in Icelandic phonology that the spirant v is a sonorant and is to be treated as a labial glide.

word-medial position if they form the last two consonants of a triconsonantal cluster.

(15)

gil.<u>dr</u>a	'trap'
hel.<u>dr</u>i	'notable (compar.)'
tim.<u>br</u>i	'timber (dat.)'
an.<u>dv</u>aka	'sleepless'
af.<u>gr</u>eiða	'help, dispatch'

For the examples in (15) we cannot appeal to vowel length as an overt indicator of syllable parsing, and it might therefore be claimed for some of the above cases that the syllable boundary should fall after two consonants (e.g. held.ri, timb.ri). However, there are good reasons to assume that the lexical syllable template of Icelandic contains no more than one postnuclear position.[5] The crucial evidence is found in the behavior of heteromorphemic triconsonantal clusters whose last two consonants cannot form an onset because of their sonority profile. In such cases, the medial consonants are lost, as in <u>kem(b)di</u> 'combed' (cf. <u>kemba</u> 'comb') or <u>hal(f)na</u> 'finish one half' (cf. <u>halfur</u> 'half'). These cases of

___

[5]See also Borowsky (1986), where the evidence from English points to the same conclusion.

consonant loss, straightforward consequences of Stray Erasure under the assumption that Icelandic permits only a single coda consonant lexically, would have no explanation if complex codas like <u>mb</u> were possible.

Thus it appears that it would be quite inappropriate to restrict the onset possibilities in Icelandic to the sequences {p,t,k,s} + {r,j,v}, and we must also admit the other clusters (with rising sonority) to be syllabified as onsets in certain cases. However, once we admit other sequences as permissible onsets, the difference in syllabification in (12a) and (12b) is unexplained.[6] I will argue below that - coupled with a language-specific tautosyllabicity constraint - the setting of the Directionality parameter (left-to-right) on syllable-mapping for Icelandic correctly predicts the desired syllabification for all the cases discussed above. As a language-specific syllable condition, I propose the tautosyllabicity condition (16) for Icelandic. This conditions works in the same way as the universal Core Syllable Condition (3). Just as the Core Syllable Condition disallows heterosyllabic parsing of CV sequences,

---

[6]It is interesting to note that this problem does not arise in the syllable boundary theory (Vennemann 1972) because the structural description of the boundary insertion rule contains the intervocalic information.
(i) $\emptyset \longrightarrow \$ \ / \ V \ \underline{\quad} \ \{p,t,k,s\} \ \{r,j,v\} \ V$

the Icelandic condition (16) ensure the tautosyllabicity of sequences of the form {p,t,k,s} + {r,j,v}.

(16) Icelandic Tautosyllabicity Condition

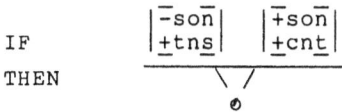

The consonants p,t,k,s and r,j,v are characterized by the feature combinations [-son, +tense] and [+cont, +son], respectively.[7] I assume the feature system proposed in Chomsky & Halle (1968) in characterizing r and the glides as [+cont] to distinguish them from l and nasals, which are [-cont].

The syllabification in (17a), where k and r are heterosyllabic, violates the Tautosyllabicity condition (16) and is therefore ruled out.

(17)

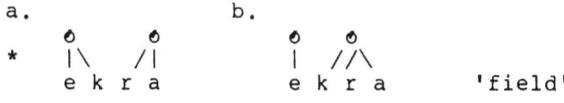

'field'

---

[7]In Icelandic, all obstruents are voiceless, and orthographic b,d,g stand for lax unaspirated voiceless stops. The segment f is [-tense] before sonorants, clusters of the form f + continuant sonorant therefore do not fall under (16).

Left-to-right directionality of syllable-mapping in Icelandic ensures that intervocalic clusters which are <u>not</u> subject to the tautosyllabicity constraint (e.g. <u>kl</u>) are syllabified as coda + onset. This is illustrated in (18).

(18) Left-to-right mapping:

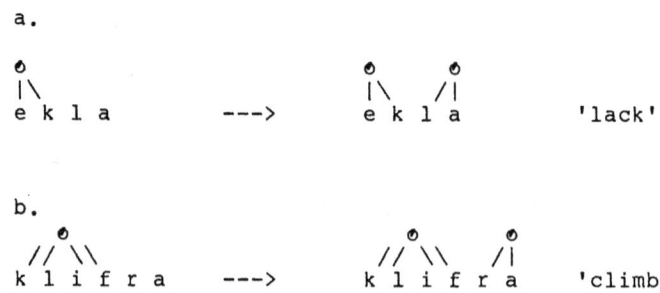

Left-to-right syllabification predicts that the sequence <u>kl</u> is split between two syllables in (18a) because the leftmost syllable is first maximized. In (18b), on the other hand, the same sequence <u>kl</u> is syllabified as the onset of the first syllable.[8] Notice that if

---

[8]Such medial clusters can, however, be tautosyllabic if the preceding syllable is already maximal. (See (15) for relevant examples.)

(i)

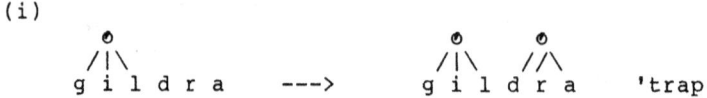

syllable-mapping proceeded from right to left, the
intervocalic k̲l̲ cluster would also be tautosyllabic:

(19)   Right-to-left mapping (hypothetical example)

a.

b.

Syllabification in Icelandic proceeds then from left
to right, maximally associating each syllable template
before the next syllable template is introduced. The
mapping is blocked if the result violates the universal
Core Syllable Condition (3) or the language-specific
tautosyllabicity condition (16).

5.1.2 Erasure and Epenthesis in Icelandic

Given the syllable analysis developed in the preceding section, let us now turn to the phonological system of Icelandic which exhibits a complex interaction of elisions (Stray Erasure) and insertions (Stray Epenthesis). Our analysis will crucially rely on the principles which have been motivated in earlier chapters.

The standard segmental analysis of Icelandic (Anderson 1974, Orešnik 1972) posits two rules: Glide Deletion (20) and u-Insertion (21).

(20) <u>Glide-Deletion</u>: $\{ \begin{smallmatrix} j \\ v \end{smallmatrix} \} \longrightarrow \emptyset \ / \ C \ \_\_ \ \{ \begin{smallmatrix} \# \\ C \end{smallmatrix} \}$

```
/bylj/    --> byl     'snowstorm [acc.sg.]'
/bylj-s/  --> byls    'snowstorm [gen.sg.]'
    (cf. bylji [acc.pl.], byljum [dat.pl.])

/krefj/   --> kref    'request [pres.ind.1.sg]'
    (cf. krefja [pres.ind.3.pl.])

/byrj/    --> byr     'wind for sailing [acc.sg.]'
    (cf. byrjum [dat.pl.])

/midj/    --> mid     'middle [nom.sg.fem.]'
    (cf. midjan [acc.sg.masc.])

/söngv/   --> söng    'song [acc.sg.]'
/söngv-s/ --> söngs   'song [gen.sg.]'
    (cf. söngva [gen.pl.], söngvum [dat.pl.]'

/mörv/    --> mör     'suet [acc.sg.]'
    (cf. mörva [gen.pl.])
```

(21) u-Insertion:[9] ∅ --> u / C___ r#

a. lifr --> lifur 'liver [nom.sg.]'
                          (cf. lifri [dat.sg.])

    akr   --> akur   'field [nom.sg.]'
                          (cf. agri [dat.sg.])

    aldr --> aldur 'age [nom.sg.]'
                          (cf. aldri [dat.sg.])

    fagr --> fagur 'beautiful [masc.nom.sg.]'
                          (cf. fagran [masc.acc.sg.])

    magr --> magur 'thin [masc.nom.sg.]'
                          (cf. magran [masc.acc.sg.])

b. dag-r   --> dagur   'day   [nom.sg.]'

    stað-r --> staður   'place   [nom.sg.]'

    harð-r --> harður   'hard   [masc.nom.sg.]'

    snarp-r --> snarpur 'rough   [masc.nom.sg.]'

    tek-r   --> tekur   'take'   [pres.ind.3.sg.]

The underlying representation of the suffix morpheme in (21b) must be -r and not -ur as shown in Anderson (1969, 1974), Orešnik (1972), Kiparsky (1984): Vowel-final stems take -r (e.g. laekni-r 'physician [nom.sg.]', snjó-r 'snow [nom.sg.]', ný-r 'new', elska-r 'loves') and

---

[9]Some of the examples of u-Insertion in underived environments (21a) are analyzed by Orešnik (1972, 1978) and Kiparsky (1984) as underlying u syncopating in certain environments.

nonepenthetic u's trigger u-Umlaut (compare (22) and
(21a)).¹⁰

(22)

akr-um	--> ökrum	'field [dat.sg.]'	(cf. akur)
aldr-um	--> öldrum	'age [dat.sg.]'	(cf. aldur)
fagr-u	--> fögru	'beautiful [masc.dat.sg.]'	(cf. fagur)
magr-u	--> mögru	'thin [masc.dat.sg.]'	(cf. magur)

The environment of Icelandic Glide Deletion: C___{#,C} suggests that the phenomenon is a classic case of Stray Erasure and does not involve a rule at all: The glides j/v cannot be syllabified in these positions and are stray-erased as illustrated in simplified form in (23a).

(23)

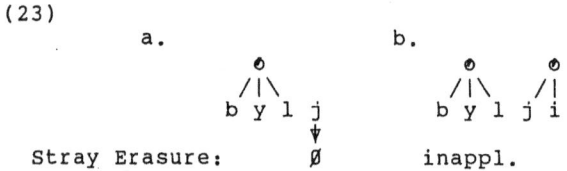

Stray Erasure: ∅   inappl.

---

¹⁰There is potentially another argument: The fact that stems which end in r do not take the -r suffix (e.g. humar 'lobster', sumar 'summer', faðir 'father') can be understood as an OCP effect if the underlying representation of the suffix morpheme is -r but not -ur.

The rule of u-Insertion can be interpreted as syllable-mapping epenthesis which is restricted to r.[11]

(24) Icelandic Syllable-Mapping Epenthesis

Associate r to the postnuclear position in the syllable template.

The application of Epenthesis (24) is illustrated in (25).

(25)

```
a.                b.                  c.                  d.
  σ                σ    σ             σ    σ              σ      σ
 /|\              /|\   |\            /|\  /|\            /|     /|\
C V C    C      C V C  V C          C V C V C           C V    C V C
| | |    |      | | |  |            | | |   |           | |    | | |
d a g  - r  ->  d a g  r     ->     d a g   r     ->    d a    g u r
                        (24)                 UCSC(3)             default-u
```

Epenthesis (24) applies to the stray r in (25a) and derives (25b). This violates the Universal Core Syllable Condition (3), therefore Structure Preservation triggers desyllabification and resyllabification of g as an onset (25c). I assume that the default values for the inserted

---

[11]We will see in the next section that in languages where epenthesis is a more general process, syllable-mapping epenthesis also falls under the Directionality parameter in many cases.

vowel are supplied postlexically, when lexical u-Umlaut no longer applies.

Individual applications of Stray Erasure and of Icelandic syllable-mapping epenthesis (24) are thus quite straightforward and require no further comment. An interesting as well as challenging situation arises for our theory when both of the stray operations are involved in a single derivation.

5.1.3 Interaction of Epenthesis and Erasure

In chapter 4 we hypothesized that both Epenthesis and Erasure are end-of-cycle operations triggered by Prosodic Licensing to eliminate stray elements from the phonological string. Stray Erasure is universal, while Epenthesis is language-specific and can be restricted in various ways (e.g. (24) which is restricted to r). From these assumptions, it follows that Epenthesis must always precede Erasure in its application, otherwise evidence for language-specific Epenthesis would never be found.[12]

---

[12]It seems that this order of application is at least implicity assumed in the literature dealing with epenthesis and Stray Erasure: The terminology often used is that epenthesis rescues the segments from Stray Erasure.

Let us then apply our model to the Icelandic examples involving interactions of Stray Erasure and Epenthesis (24). As illustrated in (26), we observe the effects of both Glide Deletion (= Stray Erasure) and u-Insertion (24) when the consonantal suffix -r is attached to a stem ending in a glide.

(26)

/bylj-r/ --> bylur   'snowstorm [nom.sg.]'
    (c.f. /bylj-ir/ --> byljir   [nom.pl.])

/krefj-r/ --> krefur   'request [pres.ind.2.sg.]'
    (c.f. /krefj-i/ --> krefji   [pres.ind.2.pl.])

/söngv-r/ --> söngur   'song [nom.sg.]'
    (c.f. /söngv-ar/ --> söngvar   [nom.pl.])

/sekkv-r/ --> sekkur   'sink [intr.pres.ind.2.sg.]'
    (c.f. /sökkv-um/ --> sökkvum   [intr.pres.ind.1.pl.])

These forms seem a priori problematic for our assumption that Epenthesis always takes place before Erasure. Consider the form /bylj-r/ in (27). When Epenthesis supplies the syllable template (27b), the glide is immediately syllabified as an onset to that syllable (27c) and Stray Erasure is inapplicable, yielding the incorrect form *byljur.

(27)
a.   b.   c.
```
      σ                  σ        σ              σ        σ
     /|\                /|\      |\             /|\      /|\
    C V C  C  C        C V C    C V C          C V C    C V C
    | | |  |  |        | | |    | | |          | | |    | | |
    b y l  j  - r  ->  b y l    j   r    ->    b y l    j   r   -> *byljur
                       Epenthesis(24)
```

Note that this problem cannot be solved by stipulating that Epenthesis follows Stray Erasure in Icelandic; this would result in eliminating both the stray j and r as in (28).[13]

(28)
a.   b.
```
      σ                    σ
     /|\                  /|\
    C V C C   C          C V C
    | | | |   |          | | |
    b y l j - r   --->   b y l    --->    *byl
            Stray
            Erasure
```

It turns out, however, that we do not need to weaken our theoretical assumptions to deal with these cases. The solution lies in cyclicity and lexical Extraprosodicity.

---

[13]Previous analyses in which special and individually ordered phonological rules are posited for deletions and insertions can resort to an ordering solution here. For example, Kiparsky (1984) proposes a syllable-based Glide Deletion rule ordered before u-Epenthesis.

Consider the cyclic derivation in (29). Each derivational step is explained below.

(29)

                    a.   b.

<u>Lexical</u>:
    Cycle 1
```
                    σ   Ex              σ   Ex
                   /|\  |              /|\  |
                   b y l j             b y l j
```

    Cycle 2:
```
                    σ        Ex
Affixation:        /|\        |          -------
                   b y l j  - r
```

Epenthesis: inapplicable
(24)

```
                    σ        Ex
                   /|\        |
Erasure:           b y l ∅  - r
```

<u>Word level</u> (no extraprosodicity):
```
                    σ                    σ
                   /|\                  /|\
                   b y l   r            b y l j
```

```
                    σ   σ
Epenthesis:        /|  /|\              inapplicable
(24)               b y l   r
```

```
                                         σ
Erasure:           inapplicable         /|\
                                        b y l ∅
```

Output: bylur   byl

-On the first cycle, the final j is extraprosodic and all segments are prosodically licensed.

-On the second cycle, the consonantal suffix -r is added in (29a), while the stem remains unaffixed in (29b).

-The stem-final j in the suffixed form (29a) loses its extraprosodic licensing. Epenthesis does not apply because the final r is now extraprosodic. At the end of the cycle, Stray Erasure eliminates the prosodically unlicensed j.

-At the word level there is no general extraprosodic licensing in Icelandic. (Recall that extraprosodic licensing at the word level is parametrized and can be restricted to certain segments, see chapter 2 for discussion.) Thus r in (29a) and j in (29b) are no longer extraprosodic. The former is subject to Epenthesis, the latter to Erasure.

While lexical Extraprosodicity is universal and hence also found in Icelandic, we are crucially assuming that in Icelandic all segments must be syllabically licensed at the word level.[14]

According to Kiparsky (1984), the Icelandic enclitic definite article is derived by postlexical morphology. For our analysis, this entails that before the enclitic is added, Epenthesis and Stray Erasure have taken place. The cliticized forms in (30) are correctly derived by

---

[14]There is a class of deverbal action nouns ending in -Cr, -Cj, derived from verb stems in -a (e.g. klifr 'climbing' from klifra 'to climb'and grenj 'wailing' from grenja 'to wail'). Kiparsky (1984) proposes to account for the fact that they do not undergo u-epenthesis or Glide Deletion by positing a postlexical morphologically conditioned rule of a-deletion. Another possibility is that the final consonants in this morphological category are specially marked by word-level Extraprosodicity. Under this assumption, the final segments are extraprosodically licensed at the word level and therefore not subject to Epenthesis or Stray Erasure. At the postlexical level there is no Extraprosodicity, but since Structure Preservation no longer holds, the Icelandic syllable structure conditions can be violated, and j and r can be adjoined to the final syllable.

adding /-inn/ to the output of the word level in (29), namely to bylur and byl.[15]

(30)

    /byl-r-inn/ --> bylurinn   *bylrinn

    /bylj-inn/ --> bylinn   *byljinn

This analysis has been possible without weakening or modifying any of our theoretical assumptions. In particular, we can maintain our hypothesis of continuous syllabification and end-of-cycle stray operations. No language-particular ordering among these mechanisms is necessary, and Stray Erasure, instead of language-particular rules of deletion, accounts for the consonant loss phenomena.

---

[15]Not all forms show the epenthetic u in the cliticized form (e.g. lifr-in). Kiparsky (1984) argues that the Strict Cycle blocks insertion of u in lifr and that cliticization bleeds epenthesis. This is not a possible solution for the theory proposed here, since epenthesis is analyzed as a type of syllable-mapping. (I am following standard assumptions in Lexical Phonology that syllable-mapping or syllabification is not subject to the Strict Cycle and can take place in underived environments.) For lifrin I will instead appeal to an independent syncope rule which deletes stem-internal vowels. Although syncope is usually not triggered by the enclitic article, Orešnik (1978) finds several cases of syncope of underlying vowels in this context (e.g. sumar, sumrin, 'summer, the summer', dŏttir, dŏttrin 'daughter, the daughter').

5.2 Further Directionality Effects

If syllable mapping is parametrized for directionality, we expect to find directionality effects in epenthesis, which is a special case of syllable mapping in our theory. This prediction is indeed borne out by several systems of epenthesis discussed in this section. The analyses will be seen to further support our hypothesis that epenthesis is syllable mapping.

5.2.1 Epenthesis in two Arabic dialects

An especially revealing case of different types of epenthesis is found in Cairene and Iraqi Arabic. The contrasting epenthesis strategies followed by these two Arabic dialects have been discussed by Broselow (1980, 1982) and Selkirk (1981).

In Cairene, a triconsonantal cluster is broken up by an epenthetic *i* between the second and the third consonant (31); in Iraqi, between the first and second consonant (32).

(31) Cairene Epenthesis: ∅ --> i / CC__C

   /ʔul-t-l-u/   -->   ʔult i lu
      'I said to him'
   /katab-t-l-u/   -->   katabt i lu
      'I wrote to him'
   /katab-t dars/   -->   katabt i dars
      'you wrote a lesson'

(32) Iraqi Epenthesis: ∅ --> i / C__CC

   /gil-t-l-a/   -->   gil i tla
      'I said to him'
   /triid ktaab/   -->   triid i ktaab
      'you want a book'
   /katab-t ma-ktuub/ -->   katab i tmaktuub
      'I wrote a letter'

After maximal syllable structure has been assigned to an intervocalic triconsonantal cluster $C_1C_2C_3$ (33), C_1 is a coda and C_3 an onset, but C_2 does not belong to any syllable.

(33)
```
      σ              σ
      |\            /|
      V C₁    C₂   C₃V
```

Selkirk (1981) argues convincingly that the difference between the two dialects is whether the stray consonant is taken as an onset or as a rime of a degenerate syllable. (Henceforth, I adopt Selkirk's (1981) terminology to refer to syllables lacking segmental nuclei as <u>degenerate syllables</u>.)

(34) Cairene

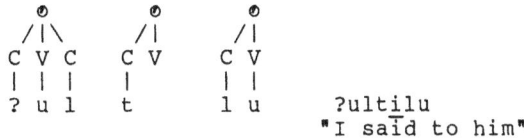

?ul t lu   ?ultilu
            "I said to him"

(35) Iraqi[16]

gil t la   gilitla
            "I said to him"

We can understand the Onset/Rime parameter, which is specifically tailored to the analysis of degenerate syllables, as a manifestation of the general prosodic principle of Directionality. Our hypothesis is that the stray consonant is mapped to the Arabic syllable template

---

[16]Note that in Iraqi, resyllabification from coda to onset is immediately triggered by the Core Syllable Condition (3), yielding the surface syllabification <u>gi.lit.la</u> from <u>gil.it.la</u>.

[CVC] from the left in Cairene (36a) and from the right in Iraqi (36b); the onset/rime difference then follows from the different setting of the directionality parameter for syllable mapping.

(36)
    a.   b.
       [C V C]   [C V C]
        :   :
        t   t

It turns out that the Directionality parameter is by no means a mere notational variant of the Onset/Rime parameter but has empirical advantages which become apparent once we go beyond the simplest instances of epenthesis.

In both the Arabic dialects discussed above, quadriconsonantal clusters are broken up between the second and third consonant.

(37)   Ø -> i/ CC__CC   (Cairene & Iraqi)
a. Cairene
    /?ul-t-l-ha/   -->   ?ult i l ha
        'I said to her'
    /katab-t-l-ha/   -->   katabt i lha
        'I wrote to her'
    /katab-t-l-gawaab/ -->   katabt i lgawaab
        'I wrote the letter'

(37cont.)

b. Iraqi

/gil-t-l-ha/ --> gilt i l ha

'I said to her'

/triid-l-ktaab/ --> triidl i ktaab

'you want the book'

/kitab-t-l-maktuub/ --> kitabt i lmaktuub

'I wrote the letter'

The directional syllable-mapping analysis extends straightforwardly to these cases. In a quadriconsonantal cluster, there are two stray consonants after initial syllabification as shown in (38).

(38)

```
    σ           σ
   |\          /|
   V C   C' C' C V
```

Syllable-mapping epenthesis supplies the Arabic syllable template [CVC] in (39), and mapping from either direction yields an intermediate heavy syllable. This explains why the two different epenthesis strategies converge on the same result in the case of quadriconsonantal clusters.

(39)

a. Cairene: Left to Right

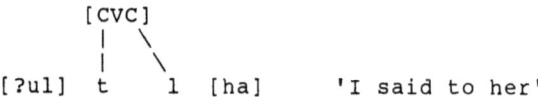

[ʔul] t l [ha]   'I said to her'

b. Iraqi: Right to Left

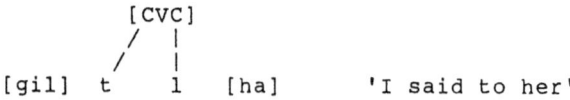

[gil] t l [ha]   'I said to her'

Notice that the Onset/Rime parameter does not by itself predict this result for quadriconsonantal clusters. For these cases, Selkirk (1981) invokes a principle which minimizes the numbers of syllables in a string (all else being equal), a rather powerful mechanism comparing possible syllabification outputs.

It is conceivable that other languages would offer further evidence for the directionality approach. Consider a hypothetical case with five intervocalic consonants, yielding three unsyllabied consonants after initial syllabification (VC]C'C'C'[CV). (The relevant cases are not attested in Iraqi or Cairene.) The directionality approach predicts that such a form will undergo epenthesis in different ways, depending on the direction of mapping: Left-to-right mapping derives (40), whereas right-to-left mapping derives (41). Notice that the outcome is uniquely determined in each case.

(40) Left-to-Right

```
        [CVC]    [CV
         | \      |
   ... l   t   r   ...              '...litri...'
         ↑      ↑
```

(41) Right-to-Left

```
         VC]   [CVC]
          |   /  |
   ... l   t   r   ...              '...iltir...'
         ↑      ↑
```

The Onset/Rime analysis, coupled with the principle of minimal number of syllables, leads to indeterminacy in such instances. It does not exclusively choose the above syllabifications, since for both (hypothetical) dialects [...litir...] is another possibility with the same number of syllables. In the directional theory, this possibility is predicted not to exist.

With six intervocalic consonants (= four unsyllabified consonants), the directionality approach predicts identical syllabifications in the two cases (see (42) and (43)), and the Onset/Rime analysis together with the minimization principle makes the same prediction.

(42) Left-to-Right

```
       [CVC]    [CVC]
        | \      | \
   ...  l  t  r  l  ...           '...litril...'
        ↑        ↑
```

(43) Right-to-Left

```
       [CVC]    [CVC]
        / |     / |
   ...  l  t  r  l  ...           '..litril...'
        ↑        ↑
```

More generally, the directional analysis predicts that if there is an even number of intervocalic consonants, the epenthetic vowel will occur at the same points in the two dialects. When the number is odd, the difference will be whether the rightmost degenerate syllable is light (left-to-right) or heavy (right-to-left).

The above considerations show that the directionality parameter alone makes unambiguous predictions in all cases, and it seems that the kind of global computational power required by the minimality principle is not necessary in the grammar.

Directionality figures prominently in tonal association, metrical structure building, association in root-and-pattern morphology, and in reduplication. These are distinct domains, and it is to be expected that the parameters are set independently.[17]

5.2.2 Comparison with a skeletal rule approach

In a skeletal rule approach, the Cairene and Iraqi epenthesis rules would be formulated so as to insert a V-slot adjacent to the stray C. The V-slot would be inserted after the stray C in Cairene (44) and before the stray C in Iraqi (45).

(44) Cairene Epenthesis: ∅ -> V / C'__

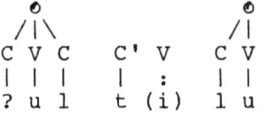

```
       o              o
      /|\            /|
     C V C    C' V  C V
     | | |    |  :  | |
     ? u l    t (i) l u      'I said to him'
```

---

[17]It is, however, noteworthy that metrical structure building in Cairene and Iraqi is governed by the same directional parameter as syllabification, left-to-right for Cairene and right-to-left for Iraqi. This parallelism is probably accidental, although further explorations may prove otherwise.

(45) Iraqi Stray Epenthesis: Ø -> V / __C'

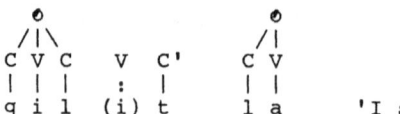   'I said to him'

In a skeletal rule approach to epenthesis, the location of the inserted vowel must be encoded in the rule. In the syllable-mapping approach proposed above in section 5.2.1, we must set the directionality of template matching. The two theories may at first appear equivalent in that one extra piece of information is needed in both cases. I will show below that the skeletal rule approach also needs to encode language-specific directionality of rule application in order to correctly account for the quadriconsonantal cases.

The analysis of the quadriconsonantal pattern of epenthesis in these Arabic dialects within a skeletal rule approach is revealing in several respects. Note first that, as shown in (46), two epenthetic vowels would be inserted when there are two stray consonants, yielding ungrammatical results.

(46)   Cairene   Iraqi

Syll:
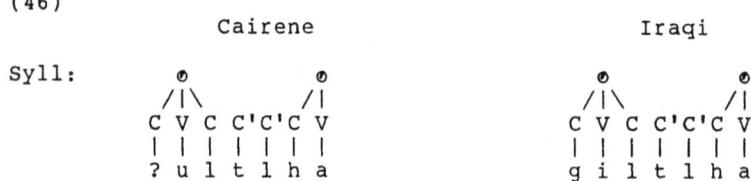

(46cont.)
Epenthesis:

This shows that epenthesis must be able to feed syllabification, providing yet another type of evidence against limiting syllable-building to once a cycle (see chapter 3). Immediate syllabification does not provide the entire solution, however. Consider the derivations in (47):

(47) a. Cairene   b. Iraqi

   [ʔul] t l [ha]   [gil] t l [ha]

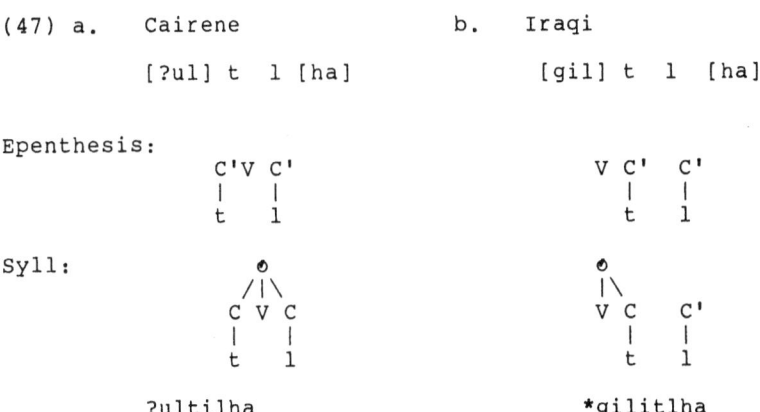

For Cairene (47a) the desired epenthesis site is found, but for Iraqi (47b) there is still an unsyllabified consonant, and a reapplication of epenthesis recreates the ungrammatical structure in (46).

Consider what happens if epenthesis applies first to the rightmost stray consonant.

(48) a. Cairene b. Iraqi

  [ʔul] t l [ha]   [gil] t l [ha]

Epenth:
```
        C'   C'V              C'V  C'
        |    |                |    |
        t    l                t    l
```

Syll:
```
              o                      o
             /|                     /|\
        C'  C V               C V C
        |    |                |    |
        t    l                t    l
```

  *ʔultliha   giltilha

Now the situation is reversed: We obtain the correct output for Iraqi (48b) but not for Cairene (48a). It seems that the skeletal rules must apply to the leftmost stray consonant in Cairene and to the rightmost one in Iraqi. Rule application must proceed directionally, and the direction is language-specific. Notice that the left-right information for a skeletal rule is needed twice, once in the structural description of the epenthesis rule, and then again in the mode of rule application. These two factors: insertion site and directionality, yield the four possible combinations diagrammed in (49). The insertion

site can be to the left or right of the stray consonant,
and rule application can proceed from the left or from
the right.

(49)

```
              |   L->R           R->L
       _C'    |                  Iraqi
              |
       C'_    |   Cairene
```

The choices for Cairene (C'__ , L->R) (50a) and those
for Iraqi (_C', R->L) (48 c) result in epenthesis in
the middle of the quadriconsonantal cluster.

(50)

    a. (C'__, L->R):   VC] C'__ C' [CV
    b. (__C', L->R):   VC] __ C'__C' [CV
    c. (__C', R->L):   VC] C'__ C' [CV
    d. (C'__, R->L):   VC] C'__ C'__ [CV

The combinations in (50b) and (50d) result in two
applications of epenthesis. If the principle of minimal
number of syllables holds true as a descriptive
generalization, such cases will never be attested in a
language with the same syllable types. This suggests that

the skeletal rule approach with its two independent left-right parameters is insufficiently restrictive.[18]

As shown in section 5.2.1, the directional syllable mapping approach to epenthesis predicts the occurrence of the attested cases of epenthesis and no others, deriving the generalization about minimal number of syllables as a theorem. Many phonological analyses proposed in the literature contain epenthesis rules applying iteratively in a directional manner, and it is to be expected that the cases involved will yield to the same sort of directional syllable mapping approach advocated here.

5.2.3 Edge epenthesis

The directional theory also makes predictions about epenthesis at domain edges. Since Extraprosodicity comes into play here as an additional factor, it is not surprising that we do not always find the same pattern as in medial epenthesis. For example, the final consonant in Cairene is extraprosodic, so that superheavy syllables [CVCC] are possible word-finally. Left-to-right mapping

---

[18]To rule out such combinations, the skeletal rule approach must resort to a convention for rule application such that if the structural change is to the right of the environment, then rule application is left-to-right and vice versa.

effects at word edges can be found in Harari, a Semitic language of Ethiopia (Leslau 1958, Kenstowicz & Kisserberth 1979:224), for which Halle & Vergnaud (1978) first offered a syllable-based approach to epenthesis.

In Harari, an epenthetic vowel [i] is inserted in the following positions:

- between the second and third consonant in a word-medial triconsonantal cluster (51a),

- between the two consonants in a word-initial cluster (51b),

- after the final consonant in a word-final cluster (51c).

(51) Harari Epenthesis

$$\emptyset \longrightarrow i\ /\ CC\_C \quad (a)$$
$$/\ \#C\_C \quad (b)$$
$$/\ CC\_\# \quad (c)$$

Word-medial epenthesis is shown in (52a), word-edge epenthesis in (52b).

(52)   root /sbr/ "break"

a. #...CCiC...#

zänsibär	/zä-n-sbär/	1pl neg imperfect
zätsibäru	/zä-t-sbär-u/	2pl neg imperfect
zäysibär	/zä-y-sbär/	3masc neg imperfect

(52cont.)

    b. #CiC...CCi#

        y<u>i</u>sábr<u>i</u>   /y-sábr/   3masc imperfect

        t<u>i</u>sábr<u>i</u>   /t-sábr/   3fem imperfect

Note that the word-medial epenthesis pattern (52a) is the same as in Cairene and results from left-to-right template matching.

Let us compare this with Iraqi word-edge epenthesis illustrated in (53).

(53) #iCC...CiC#

    a. /qmaaš/ --> <u>i</u>qmaaš (optionally <u>q</u>maaš) 'cloth'

    b. /katab-t/ --> katab<u>i</u>t   'I wrote'

For the two stray consonants at the word-edges in (52b), the left-to-right parameter also gives the correct epenthesis sites as shown below.

(54)   a. Harari (L->R)

Initial Epenthesis	Final Epenthesis
[CV	[CV
|	|
t [sáb] [ru]	- [sáb] r
t<u>i</u>sábru	-sábr<u>i</u>

(54cont.)   b. Iraqi   (R->L)

Initial Epenthesis	Final Epenthesis
VC]	VC]
|	|
q [maš]	[ka] [tab] t
iqmaaš	katabit

An initial biconsonantal cluster is split by left-to-right template matching and a final cluster by right-to-left template matching.

The full paradigm of epenthesis predicted by the directional parameter is given in (55).

(55)

	Left to Right		Right to Left	
initial	#CC -->	#CVC	#CC -->	#VCC
medial	CCC -->	CCVC	CCC -->	CVCC
final	CC# -->	CCV#	CC# -->	CVC#

5.2.4 Syllabification and Epenthesis

Our hypothesis on the relationship between normal syllabification and epenthesis is that although both are formally template mapping operations, the former is continuous throughout the derivation while the latter is an end-of-cycle operation. There is an alternative hypothesis which identifies epenthesis with syllabification, that is, full-fledged syllables with segmentally specified vocalic nuclei as well as degenerate syllables are formed in the same directional scansion. I will sketch such an approach here and consider various ramifications.

The syllabification of ʔultilu (Cairene) and gilitla (Iraqi) under the total identification hypothesis is given below.

(56) Triconsonantal Clusters:

```
                  Iraqi  R -> L    |    Cairene  L -> R
Syllab.
                    [C V C]        |      [C V C]
                     : :           |       : : :
                   g i l t l a     |      ʔ u l t l u

                    [C V C]        |      [C V C]
                     : :           |       :    =
                   g i l   t  l a  |     ʔ u l  t   l u
                            \|     |       \|/
                             σ     |        σ

                    [C V C]        |                [C V C]
                     : :           |                 : :
                   g i  l  t  l a  |     ʔ u l  t   l u
                         \|/   \|  |       \|/   \|
                          σ     σ  |        σ     σ

                   g i  l  t  l a  |     ʔ u  l  t   l u
                    \|  \|/   \|   |       \|/   \|   \|
                     σ   σ     σ   |        σ     σ    σ

Insert:            g i  l i̲ t  l a |     ʔ u  l   t i̲  l u
```

-For Iraqi, going from right to left, the first step
is to match the rightmost part of the string with
the CVC template, forming the syllable la. For
Cairene, proceeding from left to right, the initial
substring ?ul is matched with CVC.

-In the next step, the syllable template proceeds
to the middle of the string. In Iraqi, l and then
t are mapped onto the template, leaving the V-slot
open for eventual insertion. In Cairene, the medial
t is mapped, but l cannot be mapped because the Core
Syllable Condition (3) does not allow CV sequences
to belong to different syllables.

-Proceeding to the edges, the derivation is completed
by matching the leftmost substring for Iraqi and the
rightmost substring for Cairene.

Such a mapping approach, where full-fledged syllables
as well as degenerate syllables are formed on the first
directional scansion, also gives the correct parsing for
the quadriconsonantal cases as shown in (57).

(57) Quadriconsonantal clusters:

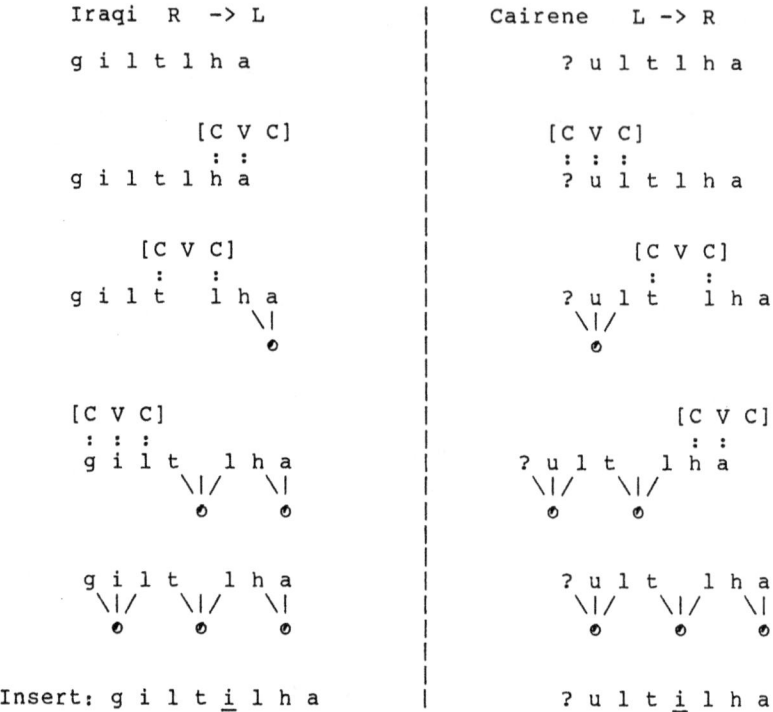

The crucial step in the directional scansion is the formation of the medial degenerate syllable. Notice that whether coming from the right as in Iraqi or from the left as in Cairene, the segments t and l are available for mapping to the [CVC] template at this point, and a closed degenerate syllable is formed in both cases.

This alternative hypothesis derives the same syllabic parsings as our end-of-cycle hypothesis, and it is quite attractive in its total identification of degenerate syllable formation with normal syllabification. The two hypotheses, however, do make different predictions about the interactions of epenthesis with other phonological rules.

Under the total identification hypothesis, no phonological rules can intervene between normal syllabification and degenerate syllable formation since the two are identified as a single syllable mapping process. This prediction is not borne out in a number of cases. For example, Melody Spread in Ponapean (discussed in chapter 4) must apply before degenerate syllable formation and therefore constitutes a serious problem. I will therefore continue to assume that degenerate syllable mapping is not to be totally identified with normal syllabification, but that it is part of the stray operations triggered by Prosodic Licensing at the end of each cycle.[19]

---

[19] Another prediction made by the total identification hypothesis is that the surface syllabic parsing of a string is the only parsing available during the derivation. This point is best illustrated by the right-to-left syllabification of the Iraqi example giltla, which is parsed as [gi.l_t.la] (see (56a)). The degenerate syllable [l_t] is heavy while the other two syllables [gi] and [la] are light, and all phonological rules which refer to syllable weight are predicted to apply to the form under this syllabification. Our end-of-cycle hypothesis, on the other hand, posits two different syllabic parsings of the string at separate stages of the derivation: [gil.t.la] before degenerate syllable formation, with a heavy initial syllable, and [gi.l_t.la] afterwards (the Core Syllable Condition ensures that resyllabification of l takes place.) The question is then whether there is evidence to support a syllabic parsing different from the surface parsing. The evidence here is not decisive. Ellen Broselow (lectures, UT Austin, 1982) points out that in Iraqi Arabic there is a difference between heavy degenerate syllables formed from quadriconsonantal clusters and light degenerate syllables formed from triconsonantal clusters: The former are visible for stress while the latter are not (see also Broselow 1982). This seems to suggest that the formation of heavy degenerate syllable is different from that of light degenerate syllables. Neither the end-of-cycle hypothesis nor the total identification hypothesis can offer an explanatory account for this problem. This is clearly an area worthy of future research.

5.2.5 Temiar epenthesis

Epenthesis in Temiar, an Austroasiatic language of the Malay Peninsula described by Benjamin (1976) and Diffloth (1976), is a regular syllabically motivated process breaking up consonant clusters.[20]

We will see that Temiar epenthesis can be understood as a result of the right-to-left matching of the syllable template CVC with one additional assumption, namely, obligatory onset mapping.

The most striking usage of epenthesis is found in the Temiar verbal system. Inflection and nominalization of biconsonantal and triconsonantal verbs is expressed by various affixational and reduplicative processes, for which McCarthy (1982) offers an insightful nonconcatenative analysis.

The language has both closed and open mid vowels, but since the latter do not appear in the examples given below, I adopt the following transcriptions for typographical convenience: [õ] = tense open mid back vowel[21], [o] = nontense open mid back vowel, [e] = nontense open mid front vowel, [@] = schwa.

---

[20] I would like to thank John McCarthy for bringing the Temiar epenthesis facts to my attention.

[21] I follow McCarthy (1982) in assuming that the distinction between the two rounded vowels is [± tense].

Phonemicized forms and their surface manifestations (with epenthetic vowels) are given in (58) - (60). The examples are various inflected and/or nominalized forms of the biconsonantal root k̄ow 'call' and the triconsonantal root slog 'sleep, marry.'

(58) #CC --> #C@C

    kn̄ow   [k@n̄ow]   active, perfective, nominalized
    trak̄ow   [t@rak̄ow]   causative, simulfactive
    slog   [s@log]   active, perfective
    snalog   [s@nalog]   active, simulfactive, nominalized
    sralog   [s@ralog]   causative, simulfactive

(59) #CCC --> #CeCC

    kwk̄ow   [kewk̄ow]   active, continuative
    kwn̄ow   [kewn̄ow]   active, continuative, nominalized
    trk̄ow   [terk̄ow]   causative, perfective
    snlog   [senlog]   active, perfective, nominalized
    sglog   [seglog]   active, continuative
    srlog   [serlog]   causative, perfective

(60)   #CCCC --> C@CeCC

    trwkōw [t@rewkōw] causative, continuative

    trnkōw [t@renkōw] causative,continuative,nominalized

    snglog [s@neglog] active, continuative, nominalized

    srglog [s@reglog] causative, continuative

    srnlog [s@renlog] causative,continuative,nominalized

An initial biconsonantal cluster is split by schwa (58), a triconsonantal cluster by [e] (59), and a quadriconsonantal cluster by both schwa and [e] (60). These facts can be straightforwardly understood as right-to-left syllable mapping of the Temiar syllable template [CVC], with the additional language-specific condition that onsets are obligatory. The nature of the inserted vowel is then determined by the resulting syllable structure, namely, schwa in open syllables and [e] in closed syllables.[22]

The only permissible syllable types in Temiar are [CVC] and [CV], onsetless syllables being disallowed. In (61a) and (61b), then, template matching is unambiguous. The stray consonant s̱ in (61a) can only be mapped to the onset position since normal as well as

---

[22]The directional idea is explicitly mentioned in Diffloth's (1976:234) statement of the rule determining the quality of the epenthetic vowel: "[...] if we count consonants backward, starting from the main vowel: /-[e]-/ is inserted in front of any consonant which is preceded and followed by another consonant. [JI]"

degenerate syllables in Temiar are governed by the onset requirement. In (61b) two stray consonants s and n are mapped onto the two positions in the [CVC] template.

(61)

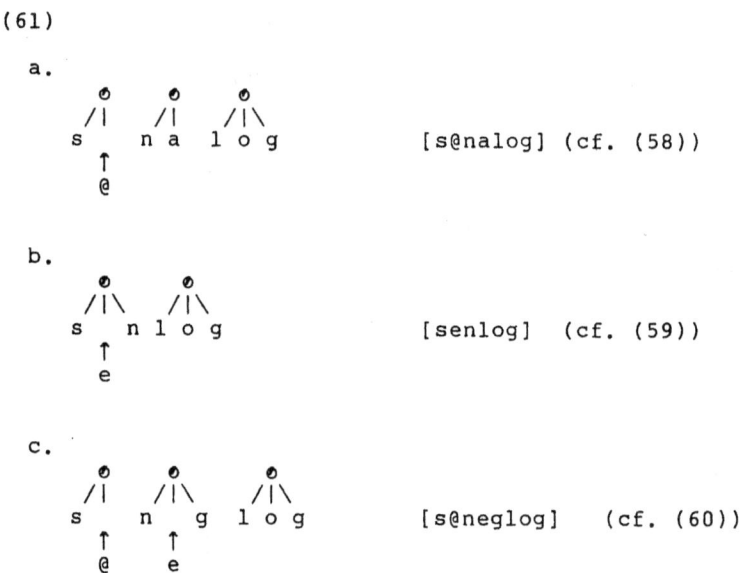

a. s n a l o g   [s@nalog] (cf. (58))
       ↑
       @

b. s n l o g   [senlog] (cf. (59))
    ↑
    e

c. s n g l o g   [s@neglog] (cf. (60))
       ↑ ↑
       @ e

In (61c), however, directionality is essential in determining the correct epenthesis sites. Right-to-left syllable mapping ensures that among the elements of the initial cluster sng the two last consonants n and g are first mapped to the syllable. Left-to-right mapping makes wrong predictions since the leftmost consonants s and n would first map to the template as shown in (62).

(62)

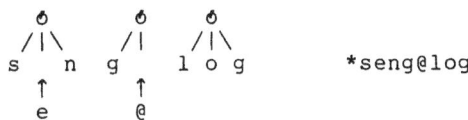   *seng@log

Note that a skeletal rule approach needs two epenthesis rules here, medial epenthesis and initial epenthesis, whose structural descriptions cannot be collapsed. The former inserts a V to the left, the latter to the right of a stray consonant. This again shows that the environment specifications of such skeletal rules are redundant with respect to the syllable structure conditions of the language, which in this case independently require syllables to have onsets.[23]

---

[23]Expressive reduplication shows apparently irregular patterns of epenthesis: by-bguy --> beyb@guy 'to waft', rg-rwēg --> regr@wēg 'to stand conspicuously upright'. There is a cyclic solution, however. On the cycle [bguy] and [rwēg], syllable mapping already yields [b@guy] and [r@wēg]. The reduplicative prefixes by- and rg- are then the only stray consonants on the reduplicative cycle and are mapped onto a single template. This is in conformity with Diffloth's (1976) observation that certain junctures block the epenthetic process.

5.3 Concluding Remarks

In this chapter, we have seen that the mapping of syllable templates to segmental strings is, like other parts of Prosodic Phonology, governed by a Directionality parameter. Clear directionality effects have been found in the syllabification and syllable-related phonology of Icelandic (section 5.1), several Arabic dialects (Cairene, Iraqi, and Harari), and Temiar (section 5.2).

It is interesting to note that directional mapping to syllable templates also plays an important role in the theory of Prosodic Morphology as developed by McCarthy and Prince (1985, in prep.), where skeletal templates with a morphological function (e.g. in reduplication) are viewed as consisting of the independently justified units of prosody (moras, syllables, feet, etc.). Since directional association is one of the factors determining reduplicative patterns, this is another area in which the directionality of the syllable-mapping process is crucial.

The overall goal of this dissertation has been to properly integrate Syllable Theory into the framework of Prosodic Phonology. Several types of evidence, when viewed in the light of the principles of Prosodic Phonology (prosodic licensing, locality, and directionality), have converged towards a theory of syllabification in which syllable structure conditions are stated in terms of templates and wellformedness conditions, thus in many ways confirming the approach to syllabification first put forth in Selkirk (1978). Our theory allows a natural account of linking phenomena in syllabification which is at the same time compatible with strict Locality. Since the template approach is able to use the universal association mechanism to assign syllable structure to strings of segments, no building rules specific to syllables are necessary. The difference between lexical and postlexical syllabification is shown to be the result of the interaction between the principle of Structure Preservation and the syllable wellformedness conditions. Finally a nonredundant and explanatory account of epenthesis phenomena is made possible by the existence of syllable templates in the grammar.

BIBLIOGRAPHY

Anderson, S. (1969) *West Scandinavian Vowel Systems and the Ordering of Phonological Rules*, Doctoral Dissertation, MIT, Cambridge, Mass.

Anderson, S. (1974) *The Organization of Phonology*, Academic Press, New York.

Archangeli, D. (1984) *Underspecification in Yawelmani Phonology and Mophology*, Doctoral Dissertation, MIT, Cambridge, Mass.

Aronoff, M. (1975) *Word Formation in Generative Grammar*. MIT Press, Cambridge, Mass.

Aronoff, M. & R. Oehrle, eds. (1984) *Language, Sound, Structure*. MIT Press, Cambridge, Mass.

Basbøll, H. (1974) "Structure consonantique du mot italien,," *Revue Romane IX*, 27-40.

Bell, A. & J.B. Hooper, eds. (1978) *Syllables and Segments*, North Holland, Amsterdam.

Bell, A. & J.B. Hooper (1978) "Issues and evidence in syllabic phonology," in Bell and Hooper (1978) 3-22.

Benjamin, G. (1976), *An Outline of Temiar Grammar*, in P. Jenner et. al. eds. (1976), 129-187.

Borer, H. and Y. Aoun, eds. (1981) *Theoretical Issues in the Grammar of Semitic Languages*, MIT Working Papers in Linguistics Vol 3.

Borowsky, T. (1986) *Topics in English Phonology*, Doctoral dissertation, University of Massachusetts, Amherst, Mass.

Broselow, E. (1980) "Syllable Structure in Two Arabic Dialects," *Studies in the Linguistic Sciences* 10.2.

Broselow, E. (1982) "On Predicting the Interaction of Stress and Epenthesis," *Glossa*, Simon Fraser University, Burnaby, B.C. 115-132.

Cairns, C.E. and M.H. Feinstein (1982) "Markedness and the Theory of Syllable Structure," Linguistic Inquiry 13, 193-226.

Chierchia, G. (1982) "An Autosegmental Theory of Raddoppiamento," NELS XI, GLSA, University of Massachusetts, Amherst.

Chierchia, G. (1983) "Length, syllabification and the phonological cycle in Italian," ms. Brown University, Providence.

Chomsky, N. & M. Halle (1968) The Sound Pattern of English, Harper & Row, New York.

Clements, G. N. (1985) "The Geometry of Phonological Features," in Phonology Yearbook 2, 225-52.

Clements, G.N. & S.J. Keyser (1983) CV Phonology: A Generative Theory of the Syllable. MIT Press, Cambridge, Mass.

Dell, F. and M. Elmedlaoui (1986) "Syllabic Consonants and Syllabification in Imdlawn Tashlhiyt Berber," Journal of African Linguistics 7: 105-130.

Diffloth, G. (1976) "Minor-Syllable Vocalism in Senoic Languages," in P. Jenner et. al. eds. (1976), 229-247.

Feinstein, M.H. (1979) "Prenasalization and Syllable Structure," Linguistic Inquiry 10, 245-278.

Fujimura, O., and J. Lovins (1978) "Syllables as Concatenative Phonetic Units," in A. Bell and J.B. Hooper, eds. (1978), 107-120.

Goldsmith, J. (1976) Autosegmental Phonology, Doctoral dissertation, MIT, Cambridge, Mass.

Grammont, M. (1933) Traité de Phonétique, Delgrave, Paris.

Guerssel, M. (1978) "A Condition on Assimilation Rules," Linguistic Analysis 20.4, 225-54.

Hale, K. (1973) "Deep-Surface Canonical Disparities in Relation to Analysis and Change: An Australian Example," Current Trends in Linguistics, Vol. 11, 401-458.

Halle, M. & J.-R. Vergnaud (1978) "Metrical Structures in Phonology," ms. MIT, Cambridge, Mass.

Halle, M. & J.-R. Vergnaud (1980) "Three Dimensional Phonology," *Journal of Linguistic Research*, 1. 83-105.

Halle, M. & J.-R. Vergnaud (forthcoming) *Three Dimensional Phonology*.

Hankamer, J. & J. Aissen (1974) "The Sonority Hierarchy," *Papers from the Parasession on Natural Phonology*, CLS, University of Chicago, Ill. 131-145

Harris, J.W. (1969) *Spanish Phonology*, MIT Press, Cambridge, Mass.

Harris, J.W. (1977) "Remarks on Diphthongization in Spanish," *Lingua* 41, 261-305.

Harris, J.W. (1983) *Syllable Structure and Stress in Spanish: A Nonlinear Analysis*, MIT Press, Cambridge, Mass.

Hayes, B. (1980) *A Metrical Theory of Stress Rules*, Doctoral dissertation, MIT, Cambridge, Mass.

Hayes, B. (1986) "Inalterability in CV Phonology," *Language* 62, 321-51.

Hayes, B. (1986b) "Assimilation as Spreading in Toba Batak," *Linguistic Inquiry* 17, 467-99.

Hooper, J.B. (1972) "The Syllable in Phonological Theory," *Language* 48, 525-540.

Hooper, J.B. (1976) *An Introduction to Natural Generative Phonology*, Academic Press, New York.

Hyman, L.M (1986) *A Theory of Phonological Weight*, Foris Publication, Dordrecht, the Netherlands.

Itô, J. (1984) "Melodic Dissimilation in Ainu," *Linguistic Inquiry* 15, 505-513.

Itô, J. & R.A. Mester (1986) "The Phonology of Voicing in Japanese, Theoretical Consequences of Morphological Accessibility," *Linguistic Inquiry* 17, 49-73.

Jenner, P. N., L.C. Thompson and S. Starosta (1976) *Austroasiatic Studies*, Part I, University Press of Hawaii, Honolulu.

Jespersen, O. (1909) <u>A Modern English Grammar on Historical Principles: Part I: Sounds and Spellings</u>, George Allen and Unwin, London; reprinted 1961.

Kahn, D. (1976) <u>Syllable-based Generalizations in English Phonology</u>, Doctoral Dissertation, MIT, Cambridge, Mass.

Kaye, J. and J. Lowenstamm (1981) "De la Syllabicité," unpubl. ms., Université du Québec à Montréal and University of Texas/Austin.

Kenstowicz, M., Y. Bader and R. Benkeddache (1982) "The Phonology of State in Kabyle Berber," ms. University of Illinois, Champaign.

Kenstowicz, M. (1984) "Syllable Structure in Modern Arabic Dialects," ms., University of Illinois.

Kenstowicz, M. & C. Kisseberth (1977) <u>Topics in Phonological Theory</u>. Academic Press, New York.

Kenstowicz, M. and C. Kisseberth (1979) <u>Generative Phonology</u>, Academic Press, New York.

Kenstowicz, M. and C. Pyle (1973) "On the Phonological Integrity of Geminate Clusters," in M. Kenstowicz and C. Kisseberth (eds.) <u>Issues in Phonological Theory</u>, The Hague: Mouton.

Keyser, S.J. (1984) "Syllable Structure in Finnish Phonology," in M. Aronoff and R. Oehrle, eds.(1984), 7-31.

Kiparsky, P. (1973) "'Elsewhere' in Phonology," in S.R. Anderson and P. Kiparsky, eds., <u>A Festschrift for Morris Halle</u>, Holt, Rinehart and Winston, New York.

Kiparsky, P. (1979) "Metrical Structure Assignment is Cyclic," <u>Linguistic Inquiry</u> 10, 421-441.

Kiparsky, P. (1981) "Remarks on the Metrical Structure of the Syllable," in W. Dressler et al., eds, <u>Phonologica 1980</u>, Innsbruck.

Kiparsky, P. (1982) "Lexical Phonology and Morphology," in I. S. Yang, ed., <u>Linguistics in the Morning Calm</u>, Linguistic Society of Korea, Hanshin, Seoul.

Kiparsky, P. (1983) "Some Consequences of Lexical Phonology," ms., MIT, Cambridge, Mass.

Kiparsky, P. (1984) "On the Lexical Phonology of Icelandic," *Nordic Prosody III*, Elert et. al. ed. University of Umea, 135-160.

Kisseberth, C. (1970) "On the Functional Unity of Phonological Rules," *Linguistic Inquiry* 1, 291-306.

Klokeid, T. (1976) *Topics in Lardil Grammar*, Doctoral Dissertation, MIT, Cambridge, Mass.

Lapointe, S. G. & M. H. Feinstein (1982) "The Role of Vowel Deletion and Epenthesis in the Assignment of Syllable Structure," in van der Hulst and Smith eds. (1982), 69-120.

Leben, W. (1973) *Suprasegmental Phonology*, Doctoral Dissertation, MIT, Cambridge, Mass.

Leslau, W. (1958) *The Verb in Harari*, University of California Publications in Semitic Philology 21, Berkeley.

Levin, J. (1983) "Reduplication and Prosodic Structure," unpublished paper, MIT, Cambridge, Mass.

Levin, J. (1985) *A Metrical Theory of Syllabicity*, Doctoral dissertation, MIT, Cambridge, Mass.

Liberman, M., and A. Prince (1977) "On Stress and Linguistic Rhythm," *Linguistic Inquiry* 8, 249-336.

Lowenstamm, J. (1981) "On the Maximal Cluster Approach to Syllable Structure," *Linguistic Inquiry* 12, 575-604.

Marantz, A. (1982) "Re Reduplication," *Linguistic Inquiry* 13.3, 435-82.

Martin, S. E. (1952) *Morphophonemics of Standard Colloquial Japanese*, Supplement to *Language*, Language Dissertation No. 47.

McCarthy, J.J. (1979a) "Stress and Syllabification," *Linguistic Inquiry* 10, 443-466.

McCarthy, J.J. (1979b) *Formal Problems in Semitic Phonology and Morphology*, Doctoral dissertation, MIT, Cambridge, Mass.

McCarthy, J.J. (1981) "A Prosodic Theory of Nonconcatenative Morphology," <u>Linguistic Inquiry</u> 12, 373-413.

McCarthy J. J. (1982) "Prosodic Templates, Morphemic Templates, and Morphemic Tier," in van der Hulst and Smith, eds. (1982), 191-224.

McCarthy, J.J. (1983) "Ponapean Reduplication," unpubl. ms., Bell Laboratories, Murray Hill, New Jersey.

McCarthy, J.J. (1985) "Features and Tiers: Semitic Root Structure Constraints Revisited," talk delivered at the University of Illinois at Urbana, Oct. 1985.

McCarthy, J.J. (1986) "OCP Effects: Gemination and Antigemination," <u>Linguistic Inquiry</u> 17.3, 207-63.

McCarthy, J.J. and A.S. Prince (1985) "Dissecting the Skeleton," paper delivered at the 1985 West Coast Conference on Formal Linguistics.

McCarthy, J.J. and A.S. Prince (in preparation) "Prosodic Morphology."

McCawley, J.D. (1968) <u>The Phonological Component of a Grammar of Japanese</u>, Mouton, The Hague.

Mester, R.A. (1986) <u>Studies in Tier Structure</u>, Doctoral dissertation, University of Massachusetts, Amherst, Mass.

Mohanan, K.P. (1981) <u>Lexical Phonology</u>, Doctoral Dissertation, MIT, Cambridge, Mass.

Mohanan, K.P. & T. Mohanan (1984) "Lexical Phonology of the Consonant System in Malayalam", <u>Linguistic Inquiry</u> 15.4, 575-602.

Myers, S. (1986) "Vowel Shortening in English," ms. University of Massachusetts, Amherst.

Noske, R. (1985) "Syllabification and Syllable Changing Processes in Yawelmani," in van der Hulst and Smith, eds., 335-362.

Orešnik, J. (1972) "On the Epenthesis rule in Modern Icelandic," <u>Arkiv för Nordisk Filologi</u> 87, 1-32.

Orešnik, J. (1978) "The Modern Icelandic Epenthesis rule revisited," <u>Arkiv för Nordisk Filologi</u> 93, 166-173.

Orešnik, J. (1985) *Studies in the Phonology and Morphology of Modern Icelandic: A Selection of essays*, Magnús Pétursson ed., Helmut Buske Verlag, Hamburg.

Payne, D.L. (1981) *The Phonology and Morphology of Axininca Campa*, Summer Institute of Linguistics Publications in Linguistics No. 66, University of Texas at Arlington.

Pesetsky, D. (1979) "Russian Morphology and Lexical Theory," ms., MIT, Cambridge, Mass.

Poser, W. (1984) *The Phonetics and Phonology of Tone and Intonation in Japanese*, Doctoral dissertation, MIT, Cambridge, Mass.

Prince, A. (1980) "A Metrical Theory of Estonian Quantity," *Linguistic Inquiry* 11, 511-562.

Prince, A. (1983) "Relating to the Grid," *Linguistic Inquiry* 14, 19-100.

Prince, A. (1984) "Phonology with Tiers," in M. Aronoff & R. Oehrle, eds. 234-244.

Rehg, K. L. and D. G. Sohl (1981) *Ponapean Reference Grammar*, The University Press of Hawaii, Honolulu, Hawaii.

Saussure, F. de (1916) *Cours de Linguistique Générale*, Payot, Paris.

Sapir, J.D. (1965) *A Grammar of Diola-Fogny*, West African Language Monographs 3, Cambridge University Press, London.

Schein, B. (1981) "Spirantization in Tigrinya," in Borer and Aoun eds.

Selkirk, E. O. (1978) "The Syllable", in van der Hulst and Smith eds. (1982), 337-384.

Selkirk, E. O. (1980) "The Role of Prosodic Categories in English Word Stress,"" *Linguistic Inquiry* 11, 563-606.

Selkirk, E. O. (1981a) "On the nature of phonological representation," in J. Anderson, J. Laver, and T. Meyers, eds., *The Cognitive Representation of Speech*, Amsterdam: North Holland.

Selkirk, E. O. (1981b) "Epenthesis and Degenerate Syllables in Cairene Arabic, " in Borer and Aoun eds., 209-232.

Selkirk, E.O. (1984a) "On the Major Class Features and Syllable Theory," in M. Aronoff & R. Oehrle, eds. (1984) 107-136.

Selkirk, E.O. (1984b) Phonology and Syntax: The Relation between Sound and Structure, MIT Press, Cambridge, Mass.

Steriade, D. (1982) Greek Prosodies and the Nature of Syllabification, Doctoral dissertation, MIT, Cambridge, Mass.

Steriade, D. (1984) "Glides and Vowels in Rumanian," Proceedings of the Berkeley Linguistic Society, vol. 10, University of California, Berkeley.

Steriade, D. and B. Schein (1984) "Geminates and Structure-Dependent Rules," in Proceedings of the West Coast Conference on Formal Linguistics, vol. 3, Stanford University, Stanford.

Steriade, D. and B. Schein (to appear) "On Geminates," Linguistic Inquiry.

Stevens, K., S.J. Keyser & H. Kawasaki (1986) "Toward a Phonetic and Phonological Theory of Redundant Features," in J. Perkell & D. Klatt (eds) Invariance and Variability in Speech Processes, Erlbaum Pub., Hillsdale, N.J.

Tateishi, K.(1986) "What is syllabified in Sino Japanese Morphemes?," ms., University of Massachusetts, Amherst.

ter Mors, C. (1985) "Empty V-Nodes and their Role in the Klamath Vowel Alternation," in van der Hulst and Smith, eds., 313-334.

Tuller, L (1981) "On Nominal Inflection in Hausa," in Thomas-Flinders, T. ed., UCLA Occasional Papers #4: Working Papers in Morphology, 117-157.

van der Hulst, H. and N. Smith, eds. (1982) The Structure of Phonological Representations, Part I and II, Foris, Dordrecht.

van der Hulst, H. and N. Smith, eds. (1985) Advances in Nonlinear Phonology, Foris, Dordrecht.

Vennemann, T. (1972) "On the Theory of Syllabic Phonology," *Linguistische Berichte* 18, 1-18.

Vogel, I. (1977) *The Syllable in Phonological Theory with Special Reference to Italian*, Doctoral dissertation, Stanford, California.

Wilkinson, K. (1986) "Syllable Structure and Lardil Phonology," ms. University of Massachusetts, Amherst.

Yip, M. (1983) "Some Problems of Syllable Structure in Axininca Campa," *Proceedings of NELS 13*, GLSA, University of Massachusetts, Amherst, Mass.

Younes, R. (1983) "The Representation of Geminate Consonants," ms., University of Texas, Austin.

For Product Safety Concerns and Information please contact our EU
representative GPSR@taylorandfrancis.com
Taylor & Francis Verlag GmbH, Kaufingerstraße 24, 80331 München, Germany

www.ingramcontent.com/pod-product-compliance
Lightning Source LLC
Chambersburg PA
CBHW071830300426
44116CB00009B/1504